VALUE BEYOND MONEY

An Exploration of The Bristol Pound
and The Building Blocks for An
Alternative Economic System

DIANA FINCH

Value Beyond Money
By Diana Finch

© Diana Finch

ISBN: 978-1-912092-30-7

First published in 2024

Published by Palavro, an imprint of
the Arkbound Foundation (Publishers)

No part of this publication may be reproduced, stored in a retrieval system, or transmitted, in any form or by any means without the prior permission of the publisher, nor be otherwise circulated in any form of binding or cover other than that in which it is published and without a similar condition being imposed on the subsequent purchaser.

Arkbound is a social enterprise that aims to promote social inclusion, community development and artistic talent. It sponsors publications by disadvantaged authors and covers issues that engage wider social concerns. Arkbound fully embraces sustainability and environmental protection. It endeavours to use material that is renewable, recyclable or sourced from sustainable forest.

Arkbound
Rogart Street Campus
4 Rogart Street
Glasgow, G40 2AA

www.arkbound.com

www.carbonbalancedprint.com
CBP2278

VALUE BEYOND MONEY

An Exploration of The Bristol Pound and The Building Blocks for An Alternative Economic System

DIANA FINCH

palavro
PUBLISHING

The publication of this book was made possible thanks to donations from many supporters through the Crowdbound platform. Diana is very grateful in particular to the following donors, who were exceptionally generous in their support:

Angela Raffle
Ben Heald
Bevis Watts, Triodos Bank
Christian Gelleri
Darius Diamond
Elizabeth Haigh
Gene Joyner
Guido de Goede
Ian Roderick
James Cole
Jonny Finch
Marina Vaucher
Mark Thurstain-Goodwin
Mike Cranney
Miles Thompson
Neil Sellers
Nick Sturge
Robin Hill
Sandro Pampallona
Tony Fish
Yoshihisa Miyazaki
Zaid Hassan
and Crowdbound

FOREWORD

By Manda Scott

If you're reading this book, then you know we're in the midst of a Meta-Crisis (or Poly-crisis, or [fill in your own large-scale-signifier] crisis) where all the most egregious errors of our late-stage consumerist culture have reached tipping points at the same time as some of the greatest of our creative achievements. Where we go from here depends on our being able radically to change course. We need to wrest the steering wheel of the bus from the fossilised claws of the old paradigm and execute a screaming handbrake turn that will not only steer us away from the cliff's edge, but direct us to a different, more flourishing future where the human and more-than-human worlds work together in service of life. We need to aim for a new horizon where a thriving ecosystem is integral to all that we are and do; where the capacity to create flows of value around and within our world is no longer attached to the toxic notion of currencies controlled by those who would see all value swept to the top of the pile, but are evenly spread, with good intent and a sense of justice and equity.

This is our challenge. If we're going to make it through, we have not only to question the existing paradigm, but to craft visions of a new horizon. Which is hard: it's almost impossible to see the toxic nature of an ocean while we're swimming in it, and even when we begin to question the not-so-metaphoric Forever Chemicals in our water, we are told There Is No Alternative and that to imagine one is unrealistic.

It takes a courageous heart to walk at a tangent to the known, to say aloud that capitalism is a dis-imagination machine, holding us in patterns of powerlessness, that we were not all born to pay bills and then die.

It takes a visionary mindset to see beyond the horizons of scarcity and separation to places of sufficiency, connection and agency. And then to do these both together, and to enact them out in the world: this is special.

But there are more reaching this place, stepping onto the edge of what Indy Johar of Dark Matter Labs calls 'Inter-Becoming' where we work and love and share value at the emergent edge of possibility, knowing that emergence into new systems is never predictable, but that we have to take the empty-handed leap and do it with all the courage and creativity we can muster.

Diana Finch has worked at the edge of Inter-Becoming for many years. The Bristol Pound project was an extraordinary act of foresight and imagination and sheer hard work on the part of so many people. It blazed a trail into the unknown and was (still is) a torch held aloft in the darkness of our collapse. Looking beyond this to what else could work better is an act of supreme courage and vision and that's where this book goes. I commend it to your attention: we all need to walk these steps and there are more of us, more of us, more of us each day.

CONTENTS

Introduction	1
The Need To Localise	9
Bristol Pound, The Early Days	24
After The Honeymoon Period	67
A Look Under The Bonnet	96
Could I Save The Bristol Pound?	109
What Next?	124
A New Project	140
Tokenomics	154
The Final Attempt to Bring Bristol Pay to Life	207
Acronyms	220
Index	222
Further reading	224
Acknowledgments	226

INTRODUCTION

I remember being in a physics class, circa 1977. I was twelve years old. We had been learning about combustion engines and how the use of fossil fuels to create energy had enabled a massive leap in both production methods and transportation. I was struck by the equation Mrs. Brookes wrote on the blackboard, showing that CO_2 was a necessary by-product of combustion. I put up my hand and asked what seemed to be an obvious question: With the amount of coal, oil and gas being burned all over the world, weren't we changing the composition of the air, and wouldn't that affect all life on Earth?

Mrs. Brookes gave me one of those scornful looks that teachers reserve for the children who ask the most annoying and stupid questions. She told me I had no idea of the size of the planet. She laughed, and said it was ridiculous to think that we humans could be having an impact on such a massive system.

Of course, by 1977 (not that I knew it at the time) there were already scientists seriously considering the negative impacts of atmospheric CO_2 emissions, not to mention many other environmental consequences of human activity—from soil erosion to holes in the ozone layer, from habitat and species loss to acid rain. It was by then five years since Donella Meadows and her colleagues had published 'Limits to Growth', which has proven surprisingly accurate in its predictions so far. I'm not sure whether Mrs. Brookes had just not heard about any of that work, or whether she had heard about it but classed it all as the ravings of cranks. Perhaps she felt that humans are safely at the apex of creation, always one step ahead and using our immense intelligence to create technological solutions to any problems that might emerge. I'd like to ask her, but it's too late now.

Roll forward twenty years, and I was much more informed about the negative impacts of our 'advanced' economies on both ecological and social systems around the world. By then I had gone to university, dropped out, and eventually gone back again a few years later. I had completed a pick 'n' mix style of degree through which I got an introduction to sociology, psychology, linguistics and philosophy. Thanks to this, I came across a number of perspectives on the history of economic development at a global level, seeing the roles of colonisation, slavery and "aid" in creating the wealth of the "developed" nations, as well as the impact of state-sponsored religion, both in undermining indigenous cultures and through creating the view that humankind had a God-given right to exploit the Earth and all other species. I was a supporter of Greenpeace and Friends of the Earth, and attended the odd CND[1] march. I tried hard to limit my negative impact on the planet in my own little ways, refilling my bottles of detergent at the local health food shop and buying organically grown food whenever possible to minimise the chemical destruction of our living soils and insect life. I chose to get around my home town of Bath mainly on foot, with my toddler on my shoulders and my baby in a sling.

By the early 2000s, I had started thinking about how

---

1   Campaign for Nuclear Disarmament

I could not only decrease my negative impact but also increase my positive impact. I volunteered my time and energy on community development projects—like saving the local infants school, which served a very deprived neighbourhood—and trying to set up a healthy living centre to address the wellbeing needs of the local community. At that point, I decided that I would never again be employed by private enterprises, whose aim was basically to make money for shareholders. Instead, I would focus my work on purpose-driven organisations that were trying to address social and ecological problems. By working in charities, I felt I could play my part in changing the world.

That feeling didn't last. Over a period of eighteen years working in non-profit organisations, initially focusing on environmental issues and later mainly on the care sector, I began to realise that all we were doing in our charities was metaphorically picking up a few broken pieces and using sticky tape to do a makeshift mend. Meanwhile, other parts of the economy were continuing to break more things. On top of that, our work was being paid for largely by trusts and foundations, many of which had amassed their wealth through the kinds of market activity that were causing the damage in the first place. And yet, the work of the third sector was always underpaid compared to either the private sector or the public sector, and most funders seemed to feel (from their comfortable board rooms) that we should be able to achieve our charitable outcomes largely through the work of unpaid volunteers.

Over those years, I lost faith in the idea that the third sector could really change the world. On the contrary, I perceived that charities, for the most part, were actually enabling the current economic system to continue on its damaging trajectory by plastering over the worst of the gaping cracks it created.

It dawned on me that the winners in the current system are seen as *generously* donating some of their wealth, through charity, so that altruistic people can try to make the world a better place. I felt that, in reality, those who are taking the cream off the top are not paying for any of the limited resources that they assert their right to extract. They are not paying for the energy and transport infrastructures that enable them to produce and transport their goods. They are not paying for the education and health systems that enable them to have a workforce. They are not considering the damage they do to the human spirit by turning people into waged slaves, cogs in the economic machine, often doing meaningless work that deprives them of joy and purpose in their lives and creates the unhappy societies that many of us live in. They are not considering the damaging outcomes of their business models, which rely on growing the consumption of their products, in turn creating landfill waste, pollution, increasing consumer debt, and furthering the entrapment of us all in this destructive global market economy.

By this stage, my views about the economy were starting to depart radically from the mainstream. Most people feel obliged to get a job, to pay their taxes, and to play an active role in the ever-growing consumer economy, which in turn creates jobs and income for others. We are told every day on the news and through the prevailing media narrative that "economic growth" is essential to generate jobs and wealth, and to drive out poverty. We are told that money "trickles down" and can "level up" disadvantaged communities. We celebrate the work of charities that are tackling the seemingly unavoidable problems that governments and local governments supposedly can't address with their apparently limited resources. We are told that if you're doing work that is personally fulfilling, then you shouldn't expect to earn loads of money too; personal fulfilment is the reward. Earning loads of money, it seems, is the appropriate reward only for the people who either create the most economic wealth, like business leaders and wealthy investors, or who keep the wheels of the great economic machine in motion, such as corporate lawyers and accountants.

I now question every single element of that view, and it is that questioning that has driven my career in recent years, culminating in this book.

It's difficult to talk about alternative economic models because our language and ways of thinking are all tied up in the same paradigm. It is likely that you have never lived in anything other than an economy where you work to earn money (unless you have massive wealth) and then spend your money on the goods and services that help you have a reasonable standard of living (compared to your peers, at least). It's also difficult to imagine what another economic model could look like or how any one of us can help to bring it about. Most of us are not rich enough, or perhaps not brave and committed enough, to simply step off the economic hamster wheel. If I give up my job, I will quickly become homeless and hungry. Soon, my inability to pay taxes or buy the things I need will see me criminalised. Living off-grid and under the radar is not for the faint-hearted, taking years of planning and making the simple process of day-to-day living challenging.

All of that said, thinking about how we could purposefully design a different economic system is vital if we are to address our global environmental and social problems. Time is running out, if we believe the climate scientists, and it will likely take centuries to shift away from the global market economy that has taken root so deeply over the last few hundred years, perhaps since the East India Company was founded in 1600. It might seem pointless to start the work of designing a new economic system; we almost certainly haven't got centuries to fix our broken one. Chaotic collapse seems to me inevitable and fairly imminent in the grand scale of human history. I'm not just talking about economic collapse, but environmental and social collapse too. And yet I can't just shrug my shoulders and give up. Anything we can do to improve our economic design might at least soften the landing and could potentially lay the foundations for a better system to be built in the future, assuming we avoid the worst-case scenario.

This book explores the work I've been involved in since 2018 as the managing director of Bristol Pound CIC, latterly known as Bristol Pay CIC. The organisation's work was focused on trying to imagine and bring about a qualitatively better economic system. For me, this field of endeavour covers two main areas. The first is about trying to minimise the negative impacts, and perhaps even create positive impacts, within the current market-based economy. This is probably what most people think of as "new economics", and is the focus of chapters one to five. The second area is far wider and tries to imagine and experiment with non-market economics, building alternative systems that can gradually shift our perceptions of value and reduce our reliance on an ever-growing globalised market. This takes up chapters six to nine. At the end of the day, it's going to take both approaches for us to adjust to living within the means of planet Earth.

CHAPTER ONE
THE NEED TO LOCALISE

In which I apply for a new job

In the spring of 2018, I saw an advertisement for a job that looked really interesting! It was for the role of managing director of Bristol Pound CIC[2]. I didn't live or work in Bristol at the time, so my knowledge of it was extremely vague. All I knew was that it operated a complementary currency scheme of some sort, which was a concept I'd come across before.

LETS and Timebanking

Living and working in Bath in the early 2000s, I'd come across both LETS (Local Exchange Trading Systems, as invented by Michael Linton) and timebanking schemes. Both of these sorts of currency run parallel to the mainstream pound sterling but are not exchangeable for it. You can't cash in your LETS units for pounds, nor can you buy them with pounds. Rather, you earn and spend your LETS units or timebanking hours completely independently of the mainstream economy.

Local people who opt to join these schemes can buy and sell their services—and goods, in the case of LETS—with fellow

---

2   A CIC is a Community Interest Company, a type of legal entity often used by social enterprises

members. In LETS, pricing is generally up to participants, although there is usually a recommended hourly rate. In timebanking, the concept is very egalitarian; one of my hours is as valuable as one of your hours, regardless of the skills we are using. The LETS units in Bath at that time were called Olivers, after the famous Bath Oliver biscuit (itself named after the Bathonian who invented them).

These currencies were appealing to me because they offered a way for people to connect and help each other. They had the potential to create a sort of income stream for people who were not in employment or who were underemployed, enabling them to use the currency to obtain goods and services that they couldn't afford with their wages or benefits. Currencies of this sort started to pop up all over the country in the 1990s and 2000s. There was a real belief that they could build community cohesion and help people who were struggling to make ends meet.

Despite the high hopes, the impact and longevity of these currencies has been limited. They tend to be started by a few highly committed volunteers who work extremely hard to get the schemes up and running. They then generally operate for a few years within an enthusiastic and committed community, after which usage gradually tends to decline and the volunteers get burnt out. The schemes then either fall into disuse or are formally closed. Sometimes there is a legacy for the schemes, with a few people in the community continuing to share their skills and resources informally, without a currency to mediate transactions or account for value.

Leaving aside the evidence as to whether these currencies have achieved their aims of building social capital, let's look at why they tend to have this short life cycle. The main aim of a currency of this type is to circulate. For that to happen, people need to be transacting, selling their goods or services and buying other goods and services. Static unspent balances are useless. Unspent balances might not immediately look like a problem. Most of us are brought up to look after our money, and to make sure we have some saved up for a rainy day. Indeed, for us as individuals it is wise to have something to fall back on. But for a currency system, if the money is just sitting in people's accounts, it's not working.

Let's imagine how the Bath Olivers scheme would work in an idealised example, with the money circulating well. Amanda has 10 Olivers in her account. On Monday, Amanda asks Betty to babysit her children for an hour so she can go for a walk with a friend. Amanda gives Betty 10 Olivers. On Tuesday, Betty asks her friend Carla, who is great at DIY, to help her put up some shelves, which takes about an hour. Betty gives the 10 Olivers to Carla. On Wednesday, Carla asks Amanda, whom she didn't know personally but found on the Bath Olivers "offers and wants" page, to cut her hair. Carla gives Amanda the 10 Olivers.

There are two key things to note from this perfect world.

First, there were only 10 Olivers in Amanda's account at the outset, and there were still 10 Olivers in her account at the end, but 30 Olivers' worth of work got done. The ratio of transactions to balances in a currency is known as the velocity. The more transactions that happen with the money over a given period of time, the higher the velocity. In other words, the velocity of the money is a measure of how much trade, or value creation, it is enabling. If Amanda had just sat on her 10 Olivers for those three days, whilst the end position would be the same from the perspective of the balances on everyone's account on Wednesday, the 30 Olivers of value would not have been created. Amanda would not have been able to go out for her walk, Betty's shelves would be lying on the floor, and Carla would still be needing that trim.

Second, there was a loop of people connected through this exchange, even though they didn't initially all know one another. Currencies need loops and networks to function. Money has to circulate round the network, especially if the Olivers, in this case, can't be bought or sold in the mainstream economy.

Let's imagine that in the Olivers scheme, all new members are given 10 Olivers, and let's say they can't go overdrawn[3]. If there are a hundred members in the scheme, that means the sum of all the Olivers in the system is 1,000. Everybody joining the scheme lays out their offers and wants. That way people can connect with each other, spending Olivers on what they need, and earning them through the goods and services they can offer. Let's imagine that one of those hundred members is offering DIY services, and another is offering hairdressing. There are also lots of people offering other goods and services, including hand-whittled wooden spoons, portrait painting, and bonsai gardening lessons. However, let's face it: we tend to need DIY and hairdressing more often and more urgently than we need hand-whittled wooden spoons, a portrait to be painted, or instruction on looking after our bonsai trees. Over time the 1,000 Olivers will flow to the DIY expert and to the hairdresser. The other well-meaning people

---

3   This is a simplification of the reality, but I want to avoid the complication of negative numbers just now. Really, LETS is a form of mutual credit where the debtors and creditors in the system all balance out to zero.

who are offering their wonderful but rather niche skills will have very few opportunities to sell their services. This is again a simplification, but it demonstrates that for loops to emerge, everyone needs to both earn and spend; the offers and wants on the market need to be matched and balanced. Without that, money will tend to pool with certain sorts of service providers. The smaller the number of members in a currency scheme, the less likely it is that the balance of offers and wants will be just right, and the more likely it is that the currency will become stagnant and the scheme will close.

There are some exceptions to this rule. When I lived in a market town in Devon as a teenager, my ability to earn money for babysitting was hampered by the very effective babysitting circle that was in operation there. In effect, the circle functioned as a very small and specific LETS, where all the members were parents in the local community and the only service on offer was childcare. It was very simple: when you joined, you were given three paper tokens, each worth one hour of childcare, and a list of the other members, with their usual availability and contact details. The circulation of the tokens worked very well because all the members sometimes needed childcare, and at other times had both enough time and the relevant skills to look after other people's children. What we can learn from this is that, where the members of a scheme all need and are able to offer the same service, the size rule doesn't matter. But there are not many services like that. It's also worth noting that for the babysitting circle to work, it had to be hyper-local; everyone in the circle was trusting someone else with the care of the little person or people most precious to them. Nobody on the circle was a complete stranger, and any breaches of trust would quickly tarnish reputations.

Back to Bath Olivers, I started to notice some strange trends emerging in the scheme. There was a feeling that there should be social justice in the world of Olivers, that trade should be in some way fairer than in the mainstream economy, and that people's time should therefore be priced at a standard rate. But members had been socialised in the mainstream world and soon some of the pricing techniques from the mainstream started to find their way into the Olivers scheme. Whilst 10 Olivers per hour was considered fair, some would charge 12 Olivers, on the basis that they had had to pay for training to develop their skill. A few might charge 14 Olivers, justified by saying that they were also having to cover the wear and tear of the tools they were using. Others might offer lower rates, hoping to make more sales, perhaps pricing themselves very competitively at 7 Olivers per hour, with the use of tools included. Gradually the Olivers marketplace changed. Instead of offering a radically fairer experience of value exchange, it was replicating some of the pernicious features of the mainstream economy.

Other problems related to the mainstream economy started to hit local currencies too. There were concerns that some traders, like painters and decorators or hairdressers, might use LETS as a way of avoiding paying tax on some of their earnings. Charities too, who had been thinking that volunteers could be rewarded with timebanking hours, found that they might fall foul of legislation around employment and tax. Indeed, HMRC[4] has been blamed for the end of

---

4   His Majesty's Revenue and Customs, the UK's tax authority.

various timebanking and LETS schemes because of fears of prosecution for tax avoidance.

What becomes of the 'money' when a LETS or timebanking scheme closes? The answer is that the closing balances are just written off because they are not exchangeable for legal tender. The main reason for that lack of exchangeability is that they are not "backed" by any assets or resources. As a result, there are winners and losers. The losers are the people who did the most work—they will have unspent, and now unusable, units on their account or tokens in their wallet, recognising the real work they did. The others are all winners, as they have received goods or services effectively for free.

It's worth saying that it's not really possible to live your whole life within LETS and timebanking currencies. They are complementary currencies in that they operate alongside, not to the exclusion of, the mainstream currency. For example, as already noted, you couldn't pay your taxes in a LETS or timebanking currency. And as Benjamin Franklin noted, taxes are one of life's certainties.

Back To The Job Advert

The role at Bristol Pound CIC sounded ideal! It was a leadership role in a non-profit organisation, which is what I had been doing for the last several years. More importantly, it was an organisation focusing on creating systemic solutions to the problems caused by our mainstream economic model—the exact thing I had been starting to think about. Plus, I thought it was bound to include lots of numbers and spreadsheets, which is absolutely my comfort zone. So, I applied.

VALUE BEYOND MONEY

A couple of interviews later, I was offered the role. I was very excited, but also somewhat nervous. I knew very little about the Bristol Pound, and even less about economics, which, throughout the interviews, I had realised was something of a gap in my education. I started on 9th July, 2018. At the end of the first week, I had begun to understand the aims of the local currency and something about its operations.

Localisation

What was the Bristol Pound trying to achieve? In broad terms, the aim was for people and businesses to buy what they needed as locally as possible. For people, this was about going to locally owned shops and, as far as possible, buying locally grown food or locally manufactured goods. For businesses, it was about choosing, wherever they could, local suppliers of the goods and services they needed to operate.

There are two reasons why localising supply is such an important idea. One is that localisation reduces transportation, supply chains, and thus CO_2 emissions. The other is that by localising we should be able to build more resilience and wealth in our communities.

Around the turn of the 21st century, if you were looking regularly at pie charts of global oil use, you might have noticed an interesting thing happen: the slice of the pie for oil used for transportation was growing. By 2003, it had become bigger than the slice of the pie representing oil used in manufacturing and production. There was also by this stage irrefutable evidence of climate change being caused by the combustion of fossil fuels. Reducing the transportation of goods is thus a key way to reduce our CO2 emissions and address climate change.

At that time people were also beginning to get concerned about "peak oil"; the idea that at some point we would reach the peak of fossil fuel extraction, after which extraction rates would decline as natural resources became depleted, with remaining resources becoming more difficult and expensive to extract. This was another reason to reduce dependency on oil, even for those who gave little thought to global warming.

Localisation meant that production and consumption of goods could be brought physically closer together. Instead of communities being reliant on imports flown and shipped from the other side of the world, communities should focus on producing what they need locally. Instead of creating national wealth by growing exports, we should focus on community wealth building by encouraging local businesses to better fulfil local needs.

When I started to look at some of what is going on, it seemed pretty obvious to me that there are plenty of transportation savings to be made if we could just organise ourselves with the aim of localisation. According to the British Meat Industry website, exports of sheep meat from the UK are around 95,000 tonnes per year. Meanwhile, the UK also imports around 100,000 tonnes a year of sheep meat. With a very slight reduction in our consumption of lamb chops and shepherd's pie, perhaps we could just stop shipping sheep meat into and out of the UK altogether.

There are other examples. In 2020, exports of dairy products from the UK totalled about £1.8 billion. That same year, we imported about £3.2 billion in dairy products. If we'd not exported those £1.8 billion, we'd only have had to import £1.4 billions' worth. The transportation savings would be the shipping of £1.8 billions' worth both in and out—a total of £3.6 billions' worth of dairy products not having to be shipped at all. Meanwhile, for the last few years, we've been exporting over £70 billion of grains (excluding rice), and importing over £20 billion. Again, if we had exported only £50 billions' worth, we wouldn't have had to import any, saving the shipping of £40 billions' worth. Admittedly, grains are not necessarily interchangeable, so some residual international trade might be needed, but we could certainly reduce the amount that is transported drastically.

If we combined these approaches with the creation of systems to enable us to plan food production to meet our needs, and if we avoided transporting foodstuffs to other countries for processing, only to transport them back again, we could avoid even more of the transportation of food around the world. In addition, if we changed our diets to align with the seasonally available produce from our own bioregions, maybe we could avoid unnecessary transportation altogether. However, this way of thinking is very top-down. It would rely on governments interfering with the free market through regulation and penalties, and financial incentives for farmers would need to operate very differently. Farms are businesses; they have to make money as well as produce food. They are therefore driven by global commodity prices, and by government incentive and subsidy schemes.

Of course, governments can and do intervene and create more impactful regulations, incentives and subsidy schemes. However, there are many reasons for governments not to be as interventionist as we might hope. First, we are broadly wedded to a free market approach in which businesses are encouraged to decide for themselves what to buy and sell to maximise their profits, with minimal red tape. The idea is that people making purchasing choices will determine which companies are successful in the marketplace. If we just let the market operate freely, we will maximise economic growth, which is generally considered to be what we need to resolve our many problems in society. It's a sort of Darwinistic approach to the economy—the fittest businesses, being those that operate best in the market, will survive and grow. Regulating any market might endanger economic growth, which is seen as dangerous. Second, exports are seen as a marker of a strong and successful economy, so any regulation that might limit exports is seen as negative. Exports are recognised as a way of bringing money into the UK economy; they provide evidence that we are strong competitors in a global market. Third, all governments are subject to lobbying by big businesses, who will always fight any state interventions that might limit their operations and profits.

The Town Pounds

Rob Hopkins, a permaculture[5] practitioner and teacher, started to explore with his students how localisation could be encouraged from a bottom-up approach instead of a top-down one. The result was the start, in 2005, of the Transition Network. This went on to underpin a growing worldwide

---

5   Permaculture is both an innovative framework for creating sustainable ways of living and a practical method of developing ecologically harmonious, efficient, and productive systems that can be used by anyone, anywhere (www.permaculture.co.uk).

movement through which people in their specific localities are coming together to meet their collective needs in every area of their lives.

The very first Transition Town was Totnes. It was here, as part of the Transition project, that the idea of a "town pound" emerged. The concept was to create a sort of special purpose money that would encourage people to shop locally. Unlike LETS and timebanking currencies, the Totnes Pound would be exchangeable with sterling; people could exchange sterling for Totnes Pounds, which would be worth exactly the same as sterling. But the Totnes Pounds would have a key restriction on their use: they could only be spent with member businesses, and the only businesses that could be members were local independent businesses. Those businesses could re-spend their Totnes Pounds, but again, only with other business members. Using the currency became a visible symbol of the community's intention to localise. All the money used to buy Totnes Pounds went into a special trust account which provided backing for the currency. If the scheme were to close, anyone with Totnes Pounds would be able to swap their notes back to sterling.

The fact that the currency was operating at a whole town level made it more feasible for trading loops to emerge. Meanwhile, because the currency was backed, there was no risk of anyone being out of pocket.

The Totnes Pound was looked at with interest by other Transition Network towns. Soon there was a Lewes Pound, a Stroud Pound and a Brixton Pound. Brixton took the idea to the next level (in collaboration with people from Bristol - see Chapter Two) and, in 2011, launched a digital version of their currency, too. Businesses could now pay their suppliers' bills online, instead of having to wander around with piles of Brixton Pounds. Also, people could pay digitally in shops via text messages from their mobile phones. This was cutting edge; at the time, the Brixton Pound provided the only way for people in Brixton to use a phone to pay for their shopping.

Resilience and Community Wealth

The financial crash of 2007-8 focused minds on economic resilience. The places that were worst hit were those most connected to the global economic system. Communities that could meet more of their needs locally, with local jobs in local businesses delivering locally sourced goods to local people, were far less affected. Places that had built their economies around jobs provided by multinational companies operating in their area—often referred to as "inward investment"—suddenly discovered that those jobs could disappear very quickly, resulting in high levels of unemployment and financial hardship.

It's worth exploring the idea of community wealth building here. Let's say a person starts a small business in their home town, which grows slowly and organically. The profits from the business stay with the business owner, who is quite likely to invest their gains in either growing the original business or starting another business nearby. The important thing is that the profits generated in the area tend to stay and get reinvested in that same area. Compare this with a fancy financial technology (fintech for short) startup funded by venture capitalists who aim to make a quick return on their investment, thereby extracting the profits from the town where the startup is based. Or compare it with inward investment from a multinational company that sets up a small base of operations in the town. They may well employ a few people locally, but the profits sit with the multinational company. That multinational may invest the profits in setting up a base in another town far away, or pay a handsome dividend to their shareholders in far-flung places.

Local Multiplier Effect and Leakage

Another key concept for the town pound currencies is the local multiplier effect. I mentioned earlier the importance of velocity for LETS. This concept is important for local currencies like the Totnes Pound, too. In effect, the Totnes Pounds were trapped circulating in a network of local traders. Each time a Totnes Pound passed from person to person or business to business, it was recognising a value creation. A pound spent in that closed network would pass hands and circulate, creating value. If one Totnes Pound was passed on once a month, it was doing 12 pounds' worth of value creation in a year. This is called the local multiplier effect. By contrast, if that pound was spent in sterling, which is a very open network, there is no guarantee that the pound would circulate locally.

Leakage is a related idea. If I spend £1 at a large chain store, a little of that—perhaps 40p (the actual amount varies depending on many factors)—might be retained in the local economy. This might be spent on wages for local staff, on rent to a local landlord, on local taxes to provide statutory services for the community, or on any locally sourced supplies. But the remaining 60p will leave the local economy. It will be spent by the company on head office staff, global supply chains, national and international taxes, as well as dividends to shareholders. Avoiding this leakage by creating a closed network thus maximises the local multiplier effect.

Where Was I?

So, I had become the Managing Director of Bristol Pound CIC and I had grasped some of the key concepts behind the currency. But I was joining the team quite late on, nearly six years after it had been launched and some nine years since the thinking had started. Indeed, it soon became apparent that I was joining when the currency was already in decline, which of course is not the best place to start the story. Up to now, I've talked about how I got to the point of starting to work for Bristol Pound CIC, but how did Bristol Pound CIC get to the point where it hired me?

There is the chronological and technical story of how the Bristol Pound was created, and how it developed over time. Perhaps more compelling, though, is the very human story of a group of people coming together with passion and energy, and the changing dynamics between them as the stresses and strains of the project took their toll. So, I will start with that.

CHAPTER TWO
BRISTOL POUND, THE EARLY DAYS

*In which we meet the founders and
the new currency is launched*

This chapter and the next are not my story. I have many people to thank for their generosity in sharing their individual accounts so that I could tell this amalgamated one. It won't be complete, as there are many former volunteers and staff who have not had the opportunity to feed into this narrative.

This is a very human story. It starts out full of vision, hope and excitement. There were amazing highs and unexpected thrills. There were long periods of happiness and joy. But the protagonists also experienced difficulties and dilemmas. There were stresses and strains. Sometimes, mistakes and misjudgements were made. People didn't always see eye to eye. Everyone involved in the project cared deeply about it and felt driven by it. And it's precisely because of that passion that certain tensions built up that could not always be happily resolved.

My aim in these chapters is not to assign blame, nor is it to air the details of painful old arguments. I have nothing but the utmost respect for everyone involved in the project. But the story would be incomplete if I only told the good bits and failed to explore the problems that ultimately resulted in the job ad that I saw that day.

One last point before I get started: all the opinions in this section came from the people I interviewed, not from myself. But I have not always attributed those opinions to specific individuals, because there is no need to say who said this or thought that, not least because, with the passing of time, many people's feelings have softened, and perspectives have shifted.

The Founders

The story starts back in early 2009. Independently of each other, a few people had been thinking about how Bristol could rebuild a more resilient economy following the economic crash of 2008, and how that resilient economy could also be better for the environment.

Let me introduce you to Chris Sunderland. Chris started his career as a biochemist, and it was this that initially brought him to Bristol. However, after ten years, he decided to change career and move to a more spiritually fulfilling role. This led him to be ordained in the Church of England. He subsequently became vicar of St Luke's, in the Barton Hill area of Bristol. He was becoming increasingly concerned with the state of both our society and the environment, feeling that working at a systemic level in cities was needed. In particular, he perceived there were four key levers to creating systemic change: finance, energy, food and governance. So he got busy on all four. He founded Project Agora, a local non-profit organisation focused on personal and spiritual development, working to enable a new generation of more aware leaders and entrepreneurs to emerge. He worked on the EarthAbbey project, helping people to develop a deep connection with the Earth. He was also a founding director of Sims Hill Shared Harvest, a project that engages volunteers in growing and sharing food, and continues its important work to this day. Later, Chris got involved in Bristol's democracy commission in the early 2000s, looking at the potential of a mayoral system to deliver a new agenda for the city. When the financial crisis hit, it seemed like an opportunity to go radical; to create a form of money that held moral as well as financial value. He had heard about the paper currencies already in operation by then in Totnes, Lewes, Brixton and Stroud, but felt these operated at a scale that could only create limited impact. Bristol had the potential to create something on an altogether different scale.

Meanwhile, Ciaran Mundy had taken a somewhat different route to reach some similar conclusions about the economy. He had also started out as a scientist—in his case, studying soil—the structure of which both determines and is determined by the health of the ecosystem. Ciaran could see that the industrialised economy was the driving force behind the continuing hollowing out of the planet's rich biodiversity through extraction, exploitation and pollution. He was an early member of Transition Bristol and soon took on a voluntary role as director. He founded various small commercial and non-profit projects, and ran community campaigns and festivals to promote causes such as energy conservation and the development of a sustainable food system. In early 2009, he set up a group called the Money and Economics Forum for Bristol. The inaugural meeting was attended by Chris[6]. The main agenda item was the potential to create a local currency for Bristol, similar to the town pounds already in operation elsewhere.

Ciaran was not a utopianist. He could see from the start that there was a high probability that such a currency would ultimately fail; it would operate for a while and then peter out. But to him, it seemed to be worth doing nonetheless. First, it would tell an important story about money and political power. It would be a way in for people wanting to understand the economy at a fundamental level—how and in whose interests it runs. Second, it had the potential to be a significant structural intervention, to make at least a short-term shift in how economic power was wielded in the city. Third, having looked at similar experiments in smaller UK towns and a range of currency projects around the world, Ciaran felt there was much to be learnt from a city-scale currency experiment in a developed economy.

After this initial meeting, Ciaran and Chris started to meet regularly to develop their ideas. They took up any opportunities they could to share their thoughts more publicly, with the aim of finding other like-minded souls who would be interested in joining them in developing a new currency for Bristol. In the summer of 2009, they spoke at a Transition Network meeting about their ideas. One of the people in the audience was Mark Burton.

Mark had been based in the midlands until shortly before this meeting. He had started out studying engineering at university, following in his father's footsteps. He then tried

---

6   The meeting was also attended by Peter Lipman, a founder of the Transition Network and a director of Sustrans, who continued to be supportive and helped the Bristol Pound team to access funding, in particular the organisation's first grant from the Tudor Trust.

a number of different jobs, at first working for a big business (and not liking that), then taking leadership roles in various small businesses. He wasn't really sure what he wanted to do with his life, but he needed whatever it was to be positive and meaningful. One day in 2007, he happened to pick up "Small is Beautiful" by E. F. Schumacher. This was a book that had been sitting unopened on his bookshelf since a lecturer at his university had recommended it to him back in 1992. As he read it, he realised it was changing his life profoundly. Here were the answers to the questions he'd been puzzling over for years; questions that seemed to be taboo. A key one was: "Why does everyone seem to think economic growth is a good thing?" So Mark started to search for projects that were experimenting with Schumacher's approach, soon discovering Transition Totnes and the Schumacher College. He quickly relocated to Totnes and enrolled at the college. The Totnes Pound had already been going for a year or so when he arrived. He loved the concept but could also see that in a small town like Totnes, a currency was unlikely to have the complexity in terms of a network of traders to make it impactful or viable in the longer term. Consequently, when Mark heard Chris and Ciaran speak at the Transition Network meeting about a currency for Bristol, he was very interested.

In autumn 2009, Chris and Ciaran presented their ideas again, this time at a conference organised by the Schumacher Institute in Bristol. Mark came up for the event and met someone else in the audience: Steve Clarke.

Born and bred in Bristol, Steve had gone to Manchester to do a degree in geography before moving to London. There he spent a decade starting and running a variety of small businesses: from importing recycled clothing from Holland, to publishing and retail. But in the early 1990s, he decided to follow a different path and studied part-time to be a lawyer. Once qualified, he moved back to Bristol and developed a specialism in contract law for large infrastructure projects. He eventually became an equity partner and team leader at the law firm Clarke Willmott.

By 2010, Steve was looking for another change. He had travelled to the disastrous COP15[7] in Copenhagen in 2009 and realised that attitudes to the environmental crisis in the business world needed to change dramatically. Through his work, he had been networking with small business owners in the city and heard first-hand how difficult life had become as the longer-term effects of the financial crisis played out. Independent shops and traders were all energised about the need to do something. Steve was also well connected with the universities in the city, where PhD research projects into local economic solutions abounded in a post-crash academic frenzy. An interest in local economics and growing concerns about the environment took him to the conference at the Schumacher Institute. Afterwards, he met up with Mark to share notes, and they both decided to get hands-on with the project.

A few weeks later, Ciaran and Chris were presenting yet again, this time at a Transition Bristol meeting. And it was at this meeting that David Hunter first heard about the project.

David's journey to that meeting was also via a career in law. David had moved to Bristol soon after completing his legal qualifications and settled down quickly, starting a family and working his way up in the legal profession, eventually

---

[7] 15th Session of the Conference of the Parties to the United Nations Framework Convention on Climate Change

VALUE BEYOND MONEY

becoming a partner at Bevan Brittan. After a few years, he realised that despite living and working in the city, he hadn't really become part of the local community because his clients were based all over the country. As a result, he decided to drop down to a four-day working week so that he could start doing some community volunteering. He happened across a copy of "The Transition Handbook", a publication put together by the Transition Network to explain their approach. The book made a big impression and he was left with the conviction that he needed to get involved in the three systems that to him seemed key to creating a positive impact on people and planet: finance, food and energy.

He started going to Transition Bristol meetings, and so found himself in the group when Ciaran and Chris were talking about their plans for a currency for Bristol. He immediately offered to get involved. Meanwhile, through another Transition Bristol connection, he became part of the steering group setting up The Community Farm at Chew Magna. At around the same time, he offered some pro bono legal support to the Bristol Energy Cooperative. He now had a role in each of the three key systems he'd identified. David cut his paid hours further to three days a week so that he could focus on these projects. Before long, he had also signed up for a Master's Degree in Sustainability and Responsibility at Ashridge Business School, following in the footsteps of many other leaders in the alternative economy movement in the South West. He left Bevan Brittan and took up a role with Bates Wells Braithwaite, a London-based law firm with a focus on organisations working for purposes other than profit.

So, here was a little team of five volunteer founders: Chris Sunderland, Ciaran Mundy, Mark Burton, Steve

Clarke and David Hunter. They started to meet fortnightly, usually at Clarke Willmott's offices, to develop their ideas. They worked very collaboratively, but roles and areas of responsibility gradually emerged. Steve headed up on governance and contractual issues with support from David, first developing the rules for the legal entity that would become Bristol Pound, then progressing to writing contracts and agreements covering the relationships with Bristol Credit Union (BCU[8], who were key to the currency as will become clear), business members, and individual members. David led overall project management, coordinating progress on all fronts. Chris administered the meetings and ensured good communications between team members. Ciaran was in charge of the money—both bringing it in and spending it. Mark was focused on design; how the currency would actually work in practice.

By August 2010 they had developed a clear shared vision and Steve, Ciaran, and Chris set up a community interest company, then called The Bristol and Bath Local Currency Scheme CIC. The name would be changed to Bristol Pound CIC in November 2011.

The decision to incorporate as a CIC was not quick or obvious. As the team started to think about formalising their work, they considered various alternatives. There was a strong draw towards setting up as a cooperative. They wanted a democratic structure; for the power behind the money to rest with the people of the city. However, at a more pragmatic level, they also wanted to be able to move quickly and develop their ideas. There was a risk that getting a wider group of people involved too early would

---

8   BCU became Great Western Credit Union, GWCU, in 2021.

make it more difficult to take decisions and make progress. And so the CIC was formed, but still with an aim to convert it to a cooperative in the medium term.

By this stage, the group had already decided on some key areas of functionality for Bristol's new money. One was that it needed to be a digital currency as well as a paper one. If the aim was to get businesses to localise their supply chains by paying them using the currency, they couldn't expect their bookkeepers to be walking around to their suppliers with envelopes full of cash. They liaised with the Brixton Pound team[9] to collaborate on designs for a digital currency.

They discovered early on that it should be possible for people to use phone text messages to make payments. This technology had already been used by M-Pesa in Kenya for a few years. There, many people didn't have bank accounts, so the ability for those without one to send and receive payments at distance was transformational. The potential to use this new approach for a local currency in the UK was very exciting. Remember, smartphones were still in the future!

There was also an idea from early on that the scheme should include a credit clearing circle, enabling businesses to trade with each other with less reliance on banks for short term loans and overdrafts.

A credit clearing circle is basically a form of mutual credit similar to the LETS schemes described in Chapter One. If Bertie's Bakery buys flour from William's Wholesalers, and William's Wholesalers buys fresh produce from Fred's Farm, and Fred's Farm (which has a little campsite and shop) buys cakes and pastries from Bertie's Bakery, assuming all the

---

9   In particular, they worked with Joshua Ryan-Collins, who later went on to be Senior Economist and Head of Finance at New Economics Foundation

bills were all for the same amount, and providing there was a system in place that allowed them to see the loop, there would be no need for any of the businesses to actually pay those bills. Instead, Bertie could mark the bill from William as paid, and also mark the invoice to Fred as paid, without having received or made a payment. This might not sound like a big deal, but if cash flow is tight and the invoiced amounts are large, Bertie might be able to avoid getting a bank overdraft to pay his bills by using the credit clearing circle. In effect, it's as if some non-bank money has been created that can help businesses settle their bills.

You might be thinking that the idea of mutual credit is just too complicated to work in practice, but there are some really impressive mutual credit schemes in operation. For example, there is Sardex, which started in Sardinia in 2009 and now boasts over 10,000 business members across Italy. In Switzerland there is the Wir Bank, which has been going since 1934, and has over 62,000 members. Both are real success stories. They have enabled significant amounts of trade that would probably not have been possible without credit creation. And they have managed to keep pace with technological developments, offering digital money and apps to stay relevant to modern businesses in an ever-changing world.

It was felt that a credit clearing circle could build trust between local businesses in Bristol, and could reduce delays in the settlement of invoices caused by difficulties in cash flow management. Ciaran and Mark were particularly keen on the credit clearing circle idea, feeling that without the power to create non-bank credit, the potential impact of a local currency on businesses would be significantly reduced.

In the event, a pragmatic approach won the day. A sterling-backed currency was seen as much easier to understand by most people, and far less risky, and therefore a much better initial proposition. It was also seen as the only model that would get through the regulatory red tape (there'll be much more on that later). The mutual credit offer, it was felt, could always be developed and added later once the main currency had built traction and credibility.

The long-term vision was huge from the outset. Running a city-scale currency might seem like a big enough aim for five people, but they were already thinking about something far bigger: they had their sights set on building something that could be replicated in cities across the UK, and potentially beyond.

At around this time, there was a presentation of the full vision at the Schumacher Institute, covering both the proposed new currency and the credit clearing scheme. This generated a great deal of interest from the Institute and from the New Economics Foundation.

Alongside working on the currency project, all the founders were continuing to do other things, not least because there was still no funding. In fact, the only person who was able to work on the project as part of something funded was Mark, and even that was only as of autumn 2010. Having completed a second master's degree at Liverpool, he enrolled on a funded action research PhD in Bristol. The focus of the PhD was local currencies, giving him the ideal opportunity to contribute his time. In fact, in spring 2012, as the workload ramped up ahead of the launch of the currency, Mark had to quit the PhD. Ultimately, Bristol Pound was more important to him than gaining academic recognition.

With all the blueprints in place, it was time to start engaging with the city and to build vital partnerships. At this point, work was separated into various fairly distinct areas. Rather than try to create one timeline combining all those areas of work, I'm going to look at them in sequence.

Small Businesses

If the currency was to be accepted and used by local businesses, building good relationships with potential members was urgent. Ciaran wanted to have at least 50 businesses on board early on, who could then help to leverage in a further 250 before the launch. Initially it was just a numbers game, but as time went on it was clear that the businesses would need to be diverse, covering different industries and sectors, if money was to circulate effectively. From the launch onwards, the plan was to double the business membership every year for at least the first five years.

In summer 2011, two new volunteer roles were created. Sarah Forrester took on the role of recruiting individual members, while Mike Lloyd-Jones was assigned the task of growing the business membership. I'll come back to Sarah in a little while.

Mike had studied Politics at Liverpool University, graduating in 2010. Whilst there, he had come across the book "Tescopoly" by Andrew Simms, which explains the profound negative effect the giant supermarket Tesco had on local businesses. As part of his course, he learned about the Transition Towns and even attended a lecture that mentioned the then brand-new Brixton Pound. It was clear to him by the time he left university that the two biggest problems facing humanity were climate change and inequality. Mike felt that he wanted to do something of significance to address these issues.

Mike moved to Bristol that autumn to do a master's degree, and in spring 2011, he found himself at a FoodCycle event at which he heard a presentation by Mike Zeidler, co-founder of Happy City (now Centre for Thriving Places). This presentation mentioned the Bristol Pound project, which sounded very inspiring. Just a few minutes later, Mike was amazed to find himself chatting to one of the founders (Mark), having bumped into him in the gents' toilets.

Mike hadn't been involved in political activism whilst at university, as he always felt that the activities and demonstrations many students spent their time on were not really achieving anything in the real world. But here at last was a practical project where he could focus his energies. Mike read the feasibility study that the Bristol Pound team had written. He was impressed. Here was a group of people who had thought things through and who had a real chance of making something work. Just weeks later, with his master's completed, Mike started volunteering every Thursday and Friday for the Bristol Pound project, whilst simultaneously undertaking a paid sales internship in London from Monday to Wednesday. In reality, he was also volunteering during his lunch breaks at work in London, calling up businesses in Bristol and booking meetings for later in the week.

Mike felt really well placed to help on the business engagement side of things. In his internship role, he was getting a fantastic grounding in sales, plus he was passionate about the project, so pitching the idea to businesses was easy. As the weeks and months went on, Mike and Ciaran honed their pitches. They wrote a take away document, laying out the benefits of joining the scheme, and Mike started posting regularly on social media to promote it. He learned quickly that businesses had no spare capacity for nice ideas; they needed to understand how the scheme could actually benefit them. The messaging needed to appeal at a pragmatic level. Mike was able to bring this perspective back to the executive team, who had been tending to assume that buying into the vision would be the main driver to getting businesses on board.

The main value proposition put to small businesses was the marketing potential of the scheme. By being a member, their business would be promoted to the users of the currency, who would all be looking for a place to spend their special Bristol money. Being a member was also a way of standing out; membership was an ethical credential that businesses could use to differentiate themselves from the large chain stores.

The independent Bristolian spirit was at its height at this time, as shown in April 2011, when a squat occupied by people protesting against a new Tesco Express store in Stokes Croft was raided by police. The ensuing riot saw both protesters and police injured and resulted in multiple arrests. So, being able to evidence your independence was important for businesses in Bristol at this time.

Two early business champions were Phil Haughton at Better Foods, a small chain of ethical grocery shops in the city, and Nigel Dyke of Alec French Architects, who went on to deliver the refurbishment of City Hall entirely in Bristol Pounds. Having two such well-known businesses on board was undoubtedly helpful in building that early credibility amongst small business owners. Other early adopters were the small local chain of Thali Cafés, @Bristol (now We The Curious) and later City Mayor George Ferguson's enterprises, including the Tobacco Factory Theatre and Café Bar.

Mike was personally aligned with his business engagement role at a deep level. He read "Tipping Point" by Malcolm Gladwell, and felt inspired by the potential to create a significant shift in the city's economy, helping local businesses and creating community wealth. Having felt somewhat looked down on by many of his friends at school and university, who perhaps didn't understand his passion around sustainability, at last here was a role where he could excel and define himself. In retrospect, Mike says that he pushed himself too hard, but at the time he felt so passionate, swept up in the energy of the many related projects all taking off around the same time, such as Bristol Energy Cooperative, CoExist and the Bristol Independents Campaign. Everyone was talking about Transition Towns and permaculture. There was a feeling of a movement coming together against the direction of travel being taken by the then coalition government; an alternative to austerity.

In early 2012, Mike's internship in London was due to come to an end, which meant he'd lack income to sustain his volunteering at Bristol Pound. But through a lucky encounter that February, he met someone from Remploy, an organisation that provides employment placement services for people with disabilities. They had funding to support the creation of jobs for people fitting a range of disability criteria. Both Mike and a fellow volunteer for Bristol Pound had qualifying conditions, and hence were able to be paid for three days a week on the minimum wage. Mike volunteered his time for the other two days a week, enabling him to focus full time on the business recruitment project.

As well as meeting new businesses, Mike needed to maintain relationships with those he'd already met, making sure they'd be ready to sign up when the moment came. Eventually all the paperwork was ready, but by this stage the launch date loomed. Mike had very little time to get the application forms completed by each business he'd met with. The forms were complicated and Mike realised his role had changed overnight; now he was doing customer support rather than sales. The administrative challenge of chasing up every single business was significant.

When it came to actually signing up, many of the businesses suddenly became more hesitant. There was a need to offer some kind of inducement, despite the fact that the organisation was trying to run on a shoestring. The team agreed that, for the first few months, they would offer a 10% bonus to businesses for each payment they accepted in Bristol Pounds. This would mean that for every £B10 a business received digitally, £B11 would be credited to their account. And, to make it easier for businesses to accept SMS text-based "TXT2Pay" payments (referred to as 'text-to-pay' from here on), every business joining the scheme would be given a free mobile phone (though it is worth noting that these were basic and cheap compared to modern smartphones).

Looking back, Mike feels that more of these kinds of incentives were needed to get businesses on board. *"We should have focused on making things better for people and businesses, instead of focusing on the soft stuff, like 'It's good and worthy!'"* he says. Perhaps that way the use of the currency could have grown to the scale where the circulation itself would have started to deliver on the promises of improving Bristol's economy.

Mike remembers these pre-launch days with affection. There was no office, just a couple of hot-desks in the Arnolfini building, kindly provided by Forum for the Future, who were keen to support the new currency. There were weekly team meetings at Clarke Willmott, attended by both the comparative newbies and the founders. These gatherings felt empowering and inclusive; everybody could bring ideas and be listened to. Energy was high and the excitement palpable.

That the team had succeeded in developing an exclusive and desirable brand for local businesses could be seen through some of the unexpected businesses that asked to join. A notable example was EasyJet. They wanted to run an exchange point at Bristol Airport, and there was a good reason to consider this proposal. If EasyJet was promoting the scheme to tourists, this could bring a significant influx of money into the scheme. And the potential benefit to tourists was that they would have the opportunity to curate a unique experience in the city, avoiding the chains that make many cities around the world feel like clones of each other. But, on balance, it was felt that accepting EasyJet would be seen as a major governance failure as it would represent a significant breach of the rules that limited membership to local independent businesses. Furthermore, to be seen as encouraging air travel was at odds with the localisation message of the currency and its aim of reducing transport-related carbon emissions.

The Co-op also asked to come on board as a member. Their governance structure made them seem less objectionable than other chain stores, but they were a national chain and therefore fell outside any reasonable application of the membership rules.

There were, however, some businesses that fell outside the official rules that Bristol Pound nonetheless decided to accept as members. Indeed, there was one particular business that was actively approached. This was FirstGroup, who ran the local buses (First Bus) and operated the railway franchise (then known as First Great Western). Clearly this was not a local independent business. However, FirstGroup's local operations offered lots of exciting potential. First, their involvement would mean that people could travel by local public transport using the currency, offering an easy way for people to try out the Bristol Pound. Second, it would mean that tourists arriving in Bristol Temple Meads could be introduced to the paper currency (as the station would host a cash exchange point) and so be encouraged to support local businesses during their visit. Third, there was the opportunity to have the Bristol Pound logo on signage in every bus, bringing the brand to a wide cross-section of the city's population. In reality, not many people actually bought their train or bus tickets with Bristol Pounds, especially after the launch of mobile phone app tickets (originally called MTickets) which were heavily discounted. Additionally, some bus drivers were suspicious of accepting the paper Bristol Pounds, because if they accepted them in error, they would be responsible for the shortfalls in their takings.

VALUE BEYOND MONEY

Bristol City Council and Local Politics

It was clear from the outset that having Bristol City Council's endorsement for the scheme would be important. Their reach and ability to promote the message would be a huge boost. Even better, if the team could persuade the council to accept payment for business rates and council tax in Bristol Pounds, it would create a feeling of legitimacy around the currency, while also having an important outlet for people and businesses to spend their Bristol Pounds. There was a problem though: taxes have to be paid with legal tender, and paper Bristol Pounds were just vouchers, a bit like book tokens. Nobody could expect the council to accept things like book tokens in payment of taxes. The conversation with Bristol City Council needed to focus on the fact that the new currency was fully backed and therefore immediately convertible to sterling.

There was another way in which having the council on board could help both the local currency and the local economy: procurement. If the council could be encouraged to pay at least some of their suppliers with Bristol Pounds, that money would recirculate in the local economy. To the team, this seemed a no-brainer.

David spoke to the procurement team at the council. They immediately saw the potential upside and were keen to tell prospective suppliers that bids committing to accepting at least some of their fees in the local currency would be well received. Unfortunately, the council's lawyers were less enthusiastic. They voiced concerns about out-of-town bidders potentially complaining that preferential treatment was being given to the local competition. At a time when

Preston Council was showing what could be done to support its local economy with a really imaginative and assertive approach to local procurement, it was a disappointment that Bristol wasn't as bold. However, in due course, the Social Value clause that formed part of the scoring process for invitations to tender was updated to say that the use of the local currency would be seen as a way of demonstrating additional social value.

The Liberal Democrats held the balance of power under the leadership of Barbara Janke (now Baroness Janke). Steve worked on the "elevator pitch", which spelled out three reasons to support the currency: first, it would shorten supply chains; second, it would help local businesses; and third, it would reduce transport-related carbon emissions. An added bonus was that the currency would help to engage local people so that they could learn more about each of those issues. This pitch was effectively a shorter version of a lengthier impact report that the team had written, with funding from the Tudor Trust, following an early successful grant application.

There was a certain amount of caution on the part of the politicians, understandably, and some frustration on the part of the Bristol Pound team at the lack of progress. Once again, luck played a part in shifting things. The BBC door-stepped Barbara one day, asking whether she was behind the local currency scheme that aimed to help local businesses. She was put in a difficult position where she basically had to endorse the scheme on the spot, which was fantastic for the project.

Meanwhile, the leadership of the council was on the cusp of change. Bristol was about to have its first elections for the new role of City Mayor. This new role would have greater autonomous power than any other in the previous model of council leadership. The Bristol Pound team needed to talk to all the potential candidates to get them on board.

The candidate who really understood the idea best, and who quickly supported it, was George Ferguson. George had come to Bristol in 1965 to attend the University of Bristol. Living in a city was a new experience for him. His father had served in the armed forces, so as a child he had moved around the UK and abroad, coming—as he says— "from no fixed abode". George quickly fell in love with the city. Yes, there were bomb sites, but the city had ambition. It was hungry to rebuild after the war.

George studied architecture and, early on, he came across a book called "The Death and Life of the Great American Cities" by Jane Jacobs. The book told the powerful story of how the author had defended her community in New York against the urban planners who were, from her perspective, undermining the city's fabric. It had a profound influence on George. He started to realise that rebuilding the city could be approached in different ways, and that the urban development then underway in Bristol was likely to damage the social fabric of the city rather than create cohesive communities. At that time, Bristol was busy building a brave new world of high-rise buildings and roads. The approach was top-down, with monoculture copycat estates being imposed on communities, as this was seen as an efficient way to house people. By the time George graduated and started practising architecture, he had decided he wanted to do the opposite. He wanted to work from the bottom up, listening to the desires of the communities, understanding their local arts and cultures, and developing bespoke solutions to their needs. This would create diverse "village" communities within the wider city.

George's drive to make a difference led him to get involved in local politics. He stood for election to the council in the 1970s and became one of Bristol's first three Liberal councillors. He retired from the political arena in 1979 to concentrate on his architectural practice, but continued to help shape the city's future. He was tempted back into local politics in 2012, becoming a leading advocate for the campaign for Bristol to be allowed to have an elected Mayor. Following the success of that campaign, George decided to stand for election himself, choosing to do so as an independent in order to be free of party policy.

George was introduced to the concept of a local currency for the city at a public gathering in St Werburgh's, where some of the Bristol Pound founders were explaining the project. Soon after, he met with James Bruges at the Watershed. James was already donating to the project to help it get off the ground, and encouraged George to become involved.

He quickly realised that the local currency idea fitted with his vision for the city. He made the commitment that, if he were elected Mayor, he would ensure that Bristol Pounds were accepted by the council in payment of taxes. Not only that, but he would take his entire salary in the currency too! Using the currency would be a great way to make the localism agenda visible and tangible, and to imbue it with a sense of fun. The Bristol Pound might help to redress the balance between the chain stores and the independent traders, and could potentially challenge the power that the big banks have over small businesses.

VALUE BEYOND MONEY

The election in November 2012 was a surprise to many. Labour's Marvin Rees brought in 31,259 votes, but George triumphed with 37,353. This was no mean feat; George had no party backing him and yet was able to get an inspiring message out to mobilise the voters. There was great excitement amongst the Bristol Pound team that someone who so clearly understood the project would be in a position of power. In retrospect, George's election was probably one of the reasons for the impressive growth in the use of the currency over the following three years.

It's worth saying that, even as Mayor, George found it difficult to get council finance officers on board with the plan to accept payments of local taxes in the new currency. There was resistance to making the administration of tax collection and reconciliation even more complicated. But, underpinned by economic arguments explaining the importance of enabling local businesses to thrive, both for resilience and for community wealth building, the officers were eventually convinced that the potential boost to Bristol's independent economy made it a worthwhile exercise. Meanwhile, work started in earnest to integrate the council's and the currency's systems to minimise the disruption to the council's accounting processes.

As time went on, George saw an impact from the Bristol Pound that was completely different from what he had at first envisaged: it put Bristol on the map! Whilst travelling around the world or entertaining VIPs, handing out Bristol Pounds as a gift from Bristol would always spark important and memorable conversations. George even presented a set of Bristol Pound notes to the Queen[10]. He also feels that the currency was a key factor in Bristol winning the competition to become the European Green Capital in 2015, as it made the city stand out for its commitment to systemic interventions to create a greener, fairer economy.

BCU and the FSA

On the operations side, whilst some of the team were researching the technical solutions to the question of how to design a digital currency, Steve got stuck into understanding the legislation that might apply to the project. It quickly became apparent to him that operating a digital currency was a government regulated activity and fell under the auspices of the Financial Services Authority (FSA)[11]. At this point, the regulatory options were limited. The Electronic Money Regulations, which sparked a wave of fintech company startups, were not passed into law until 2011. Those regulations created a range of options for any new local currency starting today that simply did not exist previously. The team came across a platform called Cyclos. This had been developed by a Dutch company called STrO (Social Trade Organisation), primarily as a platform for mutual credit operations. This seemed like a good solution for the digital currency, but there was a problem: Cyclos was not regulated. The question was: who would be an appropriate regulated partner to help deliver Bristol's digital local currency? The team identified BCU (Bristol Credit Union) and decided to approach James

---

10 The Queen was presented with a set of notes with the matching serial number 000002. The 000001 set of notes were given to the M Shed, part of Bristol Museums, where they are still on display.
11 The FSA was replaced by the FCA (Financial Conduct Authority) in 2013.

Berry, the CEO, whom they'd come across at a Transition Montpelier meeting. The idea was that Cyclos would provide the interface for currency users, and BCU would provide a regulated back-end to the system.

James Berry had grown up in a council estate on the outskirts of Liverpool in the late 1970s. Finances were tight in the family, though the young James was aware that there were plenty of others worse off. From early on, he wanted his work to help real people living in financial hardship. James was the first person from his family to go to university, though in the end he didn't finish his degree. Instead, he went to work in a call centre for Barclays Bank, in due course transitioning to a marketing role. His move to Bristol came when he got a job with Bank of Ireland. Thanks to his banking experience, in the mid-2000s he was an ideal volunteer for his local credit union—one of four operating in the city—taking on a board role as treasurer. Soon after, when Bristol's four credit unions decided to merge, James took on a paid role overseeing the merger, and then became manager of the resulting new Bristol Credit Union.

Initially, James thought the concept of a local currency for Bristol to be a *"flaky idea typical of the rather hippy Montpelier set,"* but James tells me that somehow Chris and Ciaran breached his defences. He started to see that there could well be benefits for the BCU of being involved. The majority of BCU members were on low incomes and were saving very small amounts of money, whereas the community currency participants might be from a very different demographic group. In providing accounts to currency users, he would be de-risking BCU's lending activities significantly by bringing in some wealthier members.

There was also a potential to introduce the customers of the new currency to existing BCU savings and loan products. It is interesting to note that he felt it was unlikely, on balance, that traditional credit union members would be interested in joining the currency, mainly because they did not have the breathing space to experiment with new ideas that would be of no obvious benefit to them. He was largely proven correct on that point over the following few years.

As time went on, James started to get interested in the broader aims of the currency project, such as encouraging customers to shop locally, and shortening supply chains. He began to see potential use cases even for the core BCU customers, such as setting up food cooperatives to buy food in bulk at discounted prices, and making food cheaper for the cooperative members. For this reason, he was very interested in Chris's Real Economy food co-op, which started life as a Bristol Pound project.

As James got involved, his main concern was ensuring BCU was operating within its regulatory framework. The paper currencies operating in places like Totnes were tried and tested voucher schemes that operated outside of any regulated activity. However, the concept of a digital local currency was all new. From a regulatory perspective, BCU would be taking deposits from currency users, creating a pot of money that could then be used to fund loans.

It's worth pointing out that, whilst James got the approval of the board to work with the budding currency project and act as the regulated deposit taker, this was never seen by the board as core BCU work. James worked on the currency in his own time. This included setting up internal governance processes, working through the system design in detail with the currency's founders, developing software to interface between BCU's systems and Cyclos, and, very importantly, detailing all this in complex documents for the FSA. In late 2011, when the operating design was complete, James went up to meet the FSA. To his relief and surprise, they voiced no concerns about the plans. However, their laissez faire approach was to change within a few short months.

By this stage it was clear that it would be too confusing to launch with both a currency and a credit clearing system. The credit clearing was proving difficult to explain to businesses. Worse, it risked eroding trust in the currency, because the credit clearing operation would not be backed by sterling. The currency would be called the Bristol Pound and would be launched first, and the credit clearing operation would be called Prospects, and would be launched further down the line. Other fun ideas for names had been considered, notably Bread (for the currency) and Gravy (for the credit clearing)—both words being slang for money—but these were ultimately rejected. With the name settled, work on the branding could begin, and the first competition for note designs was announced in the local media in January 2012.

In February, the Financial Times picked up on the competition and ran an article on their front page about the exciting new currency project in Bristol. Whilst this press attention was fantastic in terms of raising awareness and interest in the team's work, it also rang alarm bells at the Bank of England who, it seems, must have raised concerns with the FSA. The result was months of intense wrangling and bureaucracy for both BCU and Bristol Pound.

On the BCU side, James was quickly summoned to another meeting at the FSA, with the outcome this time being a letter saying that BCU could not act as deposit taker for the Bristol Pound, owing to several regulatory concerns that they went on to list in detail. James spent the next few months trying to address each of these concerns in turn. This required many late nights researching legal opinions on various aspects of credit union legislation and regulation, as well as drafting lengthy technical replies and travelling up to London to attend various meetings in Canary Wharf.

On the Bristol Pound side, Steve was going through a similarly tortuous correspondence with both the FSA and the Bank of England. A letter would come with questions, Steve would provide answers, then another letter would come with yet more questions, and so on. It became clear that the FSA and Bank of England didn't know how to categorise the project and were therefore very cautious in their approach to it.

Meanwhile, the Bank of England requested to meet both James and the directors of Bristol Pound CIC. Their main concern was the paper notes. And so it was that, in May 2012, a few representatives from a tiny local currency organisation travelled up to meet with the top people at the most powerful financial institution in the land. This meeting is remembered clearly by everyone who attended. Just walking into the Bank of England building was an intimidating experience, and once inside, they were thrown by the fact that all the staff wore strange pink coats. The atmosphere was very tense as they sat down round a huge table. They were introduced to the key people from the Bank, including the person responsible for issuing all the bank notes in England and Wales, and the person with overall responsibility for financial regulation. There were also representatives from the FSA, the Treasury and the Financial Services Compensation Scheme.

Steve was all geared up to answer any complicated questions they might ask about how the paper notes scheme would operate. But the meeting kicked off with a sort of parlour game. The Bank of England staff proceeded to pass round ten sterling £10 notes and asked the Bristol Pound team members to spot the counterfeit. It suddenly became clear to James that the Bank of England representatives were obsessed with paper currency design, so he quickly got out some of the sample notes that had already been printed with the winning artwork. He proudly pointed out the polymer coating and the numerous security features. Suddenly, the rather austere and serious faces softened, and a child-like excitement took hold of the meeting. Once the Bank of England team were reassured that counterfeiting was unlikely and that the scheme was fully backed by sterling, they were perfectly happy. Following the meeting, the Bank of England even published a very positive article about local currencies in their Quarterly Review!

The planned launch date of May 2012 had to be put back by several months as a result of all this regulatory work. But by late summer, the team felt they could delay no longer; the launch must happen. They set a new launch date, 19th September, by which time they felt sure all the legalese would be sorted. Then came the bombshell: a final letter from the FSA arrived on 17th September. Beneath the usual headings and introductory text, it went on to state that there were still concerns and that the scheme could not go ahead. This was nothing short of a disaster. There were anxious conversations: how could they postpone the launch at this late hour? Indeed, rather than postpone, perhaps this meant the launch could never happen; perhaps the bureaucrats had won.

But the team couldn't face postponing or cancelling the launch event after so much work had gone into it. So they took the very bold decision to launch despite the lack of approval from the FSA. It turned out to be the right call. It so happened that the Chief Secretary to the Treasurer, Sir Daniel Grian Alexander, had visited the city a few days earlier because of the impending mayoral elections. A Liberal Democrat himself, he had met with the Lib Dem candidate, Jon Rogers, who had publicly come out in favour of the currency. This meeting seemed to have a magical effect on the situation with the FSA; the day after the launch, the head of the Credit Union team at the FSA rang James to say that there were no further problems and the scheme could launch. Little did he know that it actually already had!

Technical Developments

Alongside the work on the regulatory aspects of the digital currency, there was lots to be done to develop the user interface and other digital assets needed to support the implementation of the currency, such as a website with a directory of the businesses taking part.

Initially, Mark Burton was leading on this, working closely with STrO (who developed and owned Cyclos), and Qoin (who were Cyclos's preferred contractors for creating customisations to the basic Cyclos platform). Qoin were also developing the SMS interface for the Cyclos platform to enable payments to be made by text messages. But the big concern was how Bristol Pound CIC would pay STrO and Qoin to do all this work. Luckily, the team secured a grant from The Tudor Trust just in the nick of time, enabling them to get on with the development.

This work on the payments side meant that Mark had little or no time to develop the website and directory. But in mid-2011, another person with the right skill set got involved. Time to introduce Graham Woodruff.

Graham was a software engineer working exclusively for small businesses. He liked small businesses and wanted to support them. He'd stopped shopping at supermarkets long before he came across the Bristol Pound project. Meanwhile, in his spare time, Graham was active in the Green Party and was involved in various campaigns for social justice. He'd also founded and been a director of the Bristol Drawing School.

When he came across the Bristol Pound project, the drawing school had just merged with the Royal West of England Academy (RWA), leaving him with extra time. He felt he had enough capacity to volunteer about a day a week for Bristol Pound, and soon found himself working alongside Mark. Graham was pleased that rather than being home-based, as much of his technical work was, this project gave him an opportunity to get out of the house and work as part of a team.

At this point there was no website or directory, though text-to-pay was already in beta testing. Graham had heard about community currencies and was excited to develop a website to showcase the local businesses that Mike was busy recruiting.

Graham was inspired by the counterculture nature of the

project, with local people taking back the power to create and use money outside the control of the big institutional powers. He hoped the currency would inspire people to think more deeply, to question their habits, and to shop with intention and awareness of their role as consumers, mindful of the impact they could make with their choices. He saw the paper notes in particular as an opportunity to attract and interest people. Graham's eyes light up as he tells me that *"Every Bristol Pound note was a conversation!"*

Graham volunteered regularly up to the point of the launch. Soon after, life took him to Barcelona for over six months. His later involvement in the project is picked up in Chapter Three.

With Mark working on the payments side, and Graham on the website, the other area of technical development was the creation of the link between Cyclos and BCU's systems to fulfil the requirement of having a regulated body controlling operations. James Berry took this on personally, creating a semi-automated program[12] that would run each afternoon, to reconcile the two systems by generating records in BCU's system for payments made through Cyclos and entries on Cyclos reflecting movements of sterling into and out of BCU accounts.

James hired Mark to help on some aspects of the ongoing development of this interface, which was helpful for both organisations. Mark really understood the bespoke changes to the Cyclos system which made things easier for James. Meanwhile, Mark gained some access to the payment data that the Bristol Pound team were usually unable to see because of the stringent agreement between BCU and Bristol Pound, necessitated by the FSA rules for credit unions.

---

12   The interface was built using a program called Curtains.

Following on from successfully working together, a non-disclosure agreement was created so that some Bristol Pound staff effectively became agents for BCU, enabling them to help with various aspects of customer support that otherwise would have been a constant burden on BCU. To a small extent, this also gave the Bristol Pound team an insight into the transactions that were taking place and a chance to hear the concerns that users of the currency were having.

James stresses that BCU had to be very cautious about data governance, especially after the General Data Protection Regulation (GDPR) became law. BCU's licence to operate was at stake if the FSA considered there were breaches of data regulation. But Bristol Pound staff perhaps never really understood the scrutiny James was under, and as a result, the issue of access to data was an area of constant friction. This friction tended to undermine the sense of collaboration, and perhaps made it feel as though BCU and Bristol Pound CIC were not quite on the same side.

Community and Public Engagement

Let's get back to Sarah Forrester, who joined the team initially as a volunteer alongside Mike Lloyd-Jones back in 2011. Sarah had spent some of her childhood attending a forest school, which focused its curriculum on sustainability and community living. By the age of 17, she was clear she wanted to work on the relationship between people and the environment. At university in Falmouth, she studied language as a system, and her thesis focused on the impact language has on the relationship between people and nature. A friend who read her thesis suggested she contact Forum for the Future as a way into finding a job that would build on her main area of interest. Forum for the Future suggested the volunteer role at Bristol Pound. And it was here that Mark and Ciaran helped her translate her approach to language into a systemic approach to the economy. In due course, her voluntary role became a job, and she stayed with the organisation until late 2013.

Sarah's role was to build community engagement, working alongside Chris Sunderland. The goal was to engage a thousand people before launch. This she achieved, thanks to her ability to tell a story that was deeply inspiring. That story was about creating a money system that would link people to the local businesses that served their community, to the artisans and food producers supplying those businesses, and ultimately, to the land itself. It was about giving people the power to be intentional in their purchasing decisions, and thus to create positive social and environmental impact in the economic system. Sarah pauses and chooses her words: *"The invitation was to make people's voices heard through how we spend our money, and to build a consciousness around that."*

This was something easy that anyone could do. You didn't have to sign up to be an activist or be an expert on the environment; anyone could just use this special new money and make a difference.

By the summer of 2012, with the launch looming, it was time to develop the wider communications and press work. It was at this point that Katie Finnegan-Clarke joined the team. Katie is Steve's daughter, but that was not her route in. It was Ciaran who reached out to Katie, having come across her through her activism. As a teenager, Katie had started out in anti-war protests and went on to be part of Occupy. She'd also been active in the feminist movement throughout. She'd just finished a degree in Economic Anthropology at the University of Sussex when Ciaran contacted her.

Katie credits Ciaran with pulling together an amazing team including a marketing guru and a designer[13] to support the communications work at this time. She tells me with admiration, *"Ciaran was the creative visionary. He brought street cred. He knew Massive Attack. He knew the cool designers."*

Katie ensured the tone of the communications campaign was positive, in stark contrast to the messaging from many activist movements. She explains passionately, *"Instead of 'stop this', it was about creating something new."* This fresh approach caught the eyes of many journalists and editors, and the press campaign for the launch turned out to be more successful in getting coverage than anyone could have hoped.

Meanwhile, Sarah was designing the launch event itself, which was to be held at St Nicholas market. If you don't know Bristol, St Nick's Market, as it is usually known, is the place to go if you want to support local independent traders. From street food to jewellery, from upcycled clothes to olive wood bowls—it's all there, providing a bustling and friendly refuge from the corporate city centre chain-stores. Bristol Pound's offices were appropriately just upstairs in the Corn Market building, making it an ideal venue for the launch. Just outside the Corn Market, where the outdoor market happens, are The Nails—four bronze pedestals used by traders back in the 17th century, providing the origin of the expression "cash on the nail". The Nails would provide great photo opportunities for the

---

13   Dom Lane was the marketing expert who developed the PR plan. Owen Davis was the designer for the launch comms.

event, with the Lord Mayor in his historic ceremonial garb and the brand-new money. The aim was to get people exchanging their sterling into Bristol Pounds at the event, and give them an opportunity to spend it immediately. The marketplace would showcase not only the currency, but the independent businesses too, in a celebration of all things Bristolian.

After the launch, Sarah's role shifted a bit. It was less about telling an inspirational story and more about helping people to use the currency. It focused on developing meaningful experiences for currency users, creating a community where everyone was welcome, and designing trails for people to explore and see the city in new ways.

Paper Notes

The most visible part of the Bristol Pound was of course the paper money. It was decided early on that the notes should be designed by the community. There would be an artwork competition that local people could enter, with different themes for the different value notes. The competition for the first set of notes, eventually issued in September 2012, was launched in February that year.

The competition was a huge success, with lots of entries submitted, from children, from established artists, and from amateurs who were inspired by the call-out. The Bristol Pound then held an exhibition, enthusiastically supported by the local newspaper, inviting the public to view the designs and vote on them. The eight winning images, which would become the fronts and backs of the £B1, £B5, £B10 and £B20 notes, then needed to be set within a coherent suite of branded note templates. This work was undertaken by Simon Rees of Rumba Design, and the results were beautiful.

With the design complete, it was time to find a company who could print the notes. This was no job for a copy shop down the street. The notes needed to be forgery-proof, and resilient enough to withstand being passed round repeatedly from wallet to till and from till to wallet. Orion Security Print, specialists in high-end ticket and gift card printing, provided the answer. However, the printing came at a price. I don't have bills going back to 2012, but the 54,000 notes printed in 2018 cost nearly £11,000. 35,000 of those notes had a face value of one pound, meaning that each £B1 cost a fifth of its face value to produce.

The notes each had a serial number and an expiry date. The expiry date was needed for the notes to be viewed as a voucher by the FSA. The team had decided on a three-year life span for each set. This meant that the whole competition, note design, and printing work had to be repeated in 2015 and 2018. When the new notes came out, currency users had a three-month window to swap their old notes for new notes. But inevitably many vouchers were never swapped, meaning that an amount of money was left in the bank account that backed the notes after they had expired. This could then be taken as income by Bristol Pound.

2012 Bristol Pound Notes. Above: Fronts. Below: Backs.

Why three years? This timescale seemed to be a happy balance of competing pressures. First, it would keep the risk of any problems arising from fraud or forgery low. Second, it would keep the notes fresh and create opportunities to repeat the publicity boost from the artwork competition regularly. And third, it would keep the workload just about manageable.

As the September launch day approached, the paper notes were printed and ready to go, but not much planning had gone into how people would actually obtain the paper money. Bristol Pound needed a network of businesses around the city who were willing both to sell the paper money, and to receive it. Mike realised that he was the person with the best connections to businesses in the city, so he went about recruiting any that were happy to volunteer this extra service to support the currency circulation. Not all businesses who volunteered to offer an exchange service were equally happy to receive and log paper Bristol Pounds on behalf of businesses, as this required more complicated cash management and using the text-to-pay system to credit the businesses' Bristol Pound digital accounts with the value of the deposited notes. As a result, there were two sorts of cash exchange points, called "Cash Points". This caused some confusion, as many people expected to see a machine set into a wall that would dispense Bristol Pounds.

Some Cash Points were places where you could just swap sterling for Bristol Pounds. Others were places where you could withdraw paper Bristol Pounds from your digital Bristol Pound account or (if a business) pay the paper money into your digital account.

The Launch

The run up to the launch was very exciting. Having paid for the notes to be printed, there was pretty much no money in the bank. How could such a tiny organisation be on the brink of this world-first event with so little money and so few resources? The truth is that the effort was fuelled by passion, and the entire team was running on adrenaline.

At first, nobody was sure how much local interest the

launch event would attract. But, as Mike says, there was *"an insane level of press coverage."* Arguably it was too much. The organisation's official phone number was Ciaran's, and to cope with the volume of calls, he had set up call forwarding to Skype so that other people could help him field the enquiries. Mike was astonished to answer the phone one day to Time Magazine.

It started to dawn on the team that the launch day might be really quite hectic thanks to all this media interest. Chris asked his wife Bobbie to help plan how the cash management would work on the day.

Luckily, Bobbie was a qualified accountant, at that point working for Bristol City Council. She had been living in the city since 1981, and had been involved in community projects throughout, including Sims Hill Shared Harvest. She was already well informed about Bristol Pound before Chris asked her for help; it had been a topic of conversation over dinner and breakfast for years by this time. Bobbie was captivated by the potential of a currency to localise the economy, shorten supply chains, and help us live more in tune with planet Earth—aims that she had believed in before she had heard of local currencies. But the idea that money itself could create relationships through financial transactions was not something she had thought about when focusing on the internal finances of organisations.

On the day of the launch, much to the team's surprise, there were queues down the street, and the Bristol Pounds sold fast. Bobbie's plans for the careful recording of transactions went to pot. Instead, she was frantically selling Bristol Pounds at the stall while Steve and Chris were running up and down stairs to the safe in the office, throwing in the sterling and taking out wads of Bristol Pounds to replenish her supplies. Within the first two hours, more than £5,000 worth of Bristol Pounds had been sold.

There were reporters and photographers everywhere. The team had of course been hoping that the BBC and major UK newspapers would show up, but they were surprised to see TV crews from around the world, including France, Spain, the USA, and even China. Chris did an interview with the Chinese state television company. Their first question was what the authorities thought about Bristol Pound and seemed surprised to hear that they were supporting the currency. After recording the interview, he asked how many people would see it. The answer? About two billion.

Local radio stations were covering the event too, and not just Bristolian local radio. Steve remembers doing an interview with a local radio station from Wolverhampton. The interviewer pitched the idea of creating their own local currency, asking his listeners to suggest potential names. The winning suggestion was 'The Noddy', after Noddy Holder from the pop group Slade, which Steve enthusiastically endorsed.

In the first few weeks after the launch, the energy and excitement continued. All the contributors to this chapter remember it fondly. There was dynamism and momentum. The team felt united and exhilarated. They were getting amazing levels of interest from the media and the general public, and were not encountering any negativity or difficult questions.

The team were all using the new currency, of course, and all had digital accounts. Bobbie remembers starting to use text-to-pay, changing where she shopped and had coffee so that she could support the new phone-based payment method.

James similarly says his personal purchasing habits changed considerably after the launch.

With so much of the publicity focusing on the paper money, there was a need to find a way to promote the digital currency, which was far less visible. The directors decided to offer a 10% uplift on the first £50,000 transferred to digital Bristol Pound accounts to incentivise people to set up digital accounts. During this promotion, If you paid £100 into your Bristol Pound account, it was credited with £110. BCU, understandably, needed to know that if everyone decided they wanted to convert their Bristol Pounds back into sterling, it would be able to make those payments without being out of pocket. The offer therefore needed a guarantee from the directors for £5,000 to cover any potential shortfall. It wasn't only their time that the directors contributed in the early days, but their hard-earned cash, too! They need not have worried though; when the first round of notes expired in 2015, £40,000 of income was generated (explained in Chapter Four), easily covering the directors' guarantee.

The person whose lifestyle was most impacted by the new currency was George Ferguson. As soon as he was elected Mayor, he was true to his word, taking his entire salary in Bristol Pounds, and doing all his shopping using the currency. This necessitated convincing loads of shops and businesses to accept it. In this way, his personal decision about how his salary was paid really helped drive early adoption by a lot of shops and businesses. George not only found the directory of businesses useful, but he helped to grow it! The Tobacco Factory was the first place in North Street to join up. This had been part of the old Imperial Tobacco Factory, which

VALUE BEYOND MONEY

George had saved from demolition and converted into a thriving cultural venue, offering a theatre and café bar, as well as hosting a performing arts school, independent markets and office spaces. Soon they were not only taking customer payments in the currency, but providing Bristol Pound 'banking' services to other businesses on the street.

By December 2012, over £60,000 in paper Bristol Pounds had been purchased, and the digital currency had a combined business and individual membership of over 500 users.

CHAPTER THREE
AFTER THE HONEYMOON PERIOD

In which things get more difficult

Rather lazily, I'm going to refer to the Bristol Pound team as "we" from here on. I know I wasn't part of the team yet, but it feels very awkward to avoid using a pronoun, and my subsequent work with the organisation makes "they" feel wrong.

The Bristol Pound story so far is truly impressive. This tiny group of people with very limited resources have launched a ground-breaking city-wide local currency, attracting media interest from all over the world. They have been mainly volunteering and are all very out of pocket as a result. They've been working extremely hard, in many cases for years.

After that success, the reality of trying to grow and manage a local currency started to kick in. This chapter is rather more downbeat as it focuses on the problems that emerged, but I don't want you to think it was all bad. So, I'll start off with a recognition of the great work that was happening to try to grow Bristol's new currency and the positive feelings that surrounded it.

VALUE BEYOND MONEY

The Bristol Pound Success Story

Jen Green, finance assistant from 2013 to 2016, shared with me some of her memories about the engagement events that were happening regularly during her time with the organisation. There was the weekly Bristol Pound stall at the Farmers Market, which always sparked lots of interest and intense conversations. There were the St Nicholas Night Markets, key to promoting the currency and which, once a year, doubled as Bristol Pound's birthday party—complete with birthday cake and much celebrating. And then there were a host of community events where the team would pitch up with a stall. Jen remembers positive receptions whenever the team was out and about at markets and events.

After the launch, Ciaran, Mike Lloyd-Jones, Sarah Forrester, and Katie Finnegan-Clarke were the core team, constantly out there, promoting and supporting the new currency.

People were talking about the Bristol Pound all over the world, and our inbox was full of international correspondence. Academics and students approached us (and still do) because we were seen as pioneering practitioners in the field of local currencies. Teachers contacted us wanting us to help them explain the negative impacts of the global market economy to their pupils. We created a range of resources for schools as a result. Councils got in touch to find out about how to support their local economy through digital payments, following our innovative approach. Activists wanted to copy what we were doing and start their own schemes. We hadn't just created a local currency; we'd sparked a world-wide awareness of the problems with our economic system.

Meanwhile, in Bristol itself, we were influencing more people every day as they joined up and started using the currency. And we were changing attitudes at the city council about the importance of local businesses within our economy.

There was a feeling that we were really changing the paradigm and creating a massive impact. The team was on a high much of the time, working hard together but having fun together too, buoyed up by the feelings of success.

Grant Funding

Work had been going on to raise funds for the development of the project since the outset. By the end of 2012, the organisation had raised just over £58,000 in grant funding. Early funders included the Tudor Trust, whose grant had mainly been spent on work with STrO and Qoin, and on printing the first issue of Bristol Pound notes. A little money had come in from Remploy too, covering part-time minimum wage salaries that enabled two of the volunteers to become employees and be paid for at least some of their time. However, the majority of the work was being done entirely on a voluntary basis. Now that the currency was launched, there was a need to create a robust operation, and that would require staffing.

There is a problem with grant funding. Funders generally want to fund something new. They tend to be less keen to fund the running costs of an existing operation. As a result, finding money to develop the Bristol Pound was extremely difficult. In 2013 we were lucky. The New Economics Foundation provided £50,000 of funding to develop the currency, which enabled us to commit to a little more paid staff time. We had some modest grants from Bristol City Council over the years that helped a bit too. We also received some money from the Centre for Sustainable Energy to encourage Bristol Pound users to switch to a green energy provider. But all this was still not enough to pay everyone for all their time. Beyond these grants, however, the team was only successful in bringing money in for new areas of work. For example, Chris put in an application to National Lottery Awards for All to fund the Real Economy, a new food cooperative project that in due course would split off into its own cooperative legal entity.

The majority of the fundraising effort in 2013 went towards a major bid to an EU funding stream called DigiPay4Growth. This bid was being led by STrO, and was framed as a research project to look at different approaches to implementing mutual credit. The bid was successful, and the project started in January 2014. At last decent money would be coming in, just over £300,000 in all, and the organisation would be able to pay people for most of the work they were already doing. The only problem was that there was little capacity to actually deliver on the mutual credit aims of the grant funding. Worse, a number of the staff and directors didn't really understand what the DigiPay money was actually for.

After the DigiPay project, we managed to bring in another large grant, this time totalling about £560,000, from Partners for a New Economy (P4NE). Again, a key focus of this funding was on developing interest-free credit for business members. Once again, the organisation was unable to devote sufficient resource to that development work, as the operational needs of the main Bristol Pound project were too great. As a result, at the end of the first grant from P4NE, further funding was not forthcoming from them.

Other grants that came in between 2014 and 2017 were also mainly linked to specific outcomes, such as developing technology that could be used by other local currencies in the UK, and enabling local currency groups across the country to liaise and learn from each other. This constant pressure to deliver on funders' goals, whilst in reality having to support the main Bristol Pound operation, led to time being spread very thinly. Team members were coping with many competing pressures and demands, often with little understanding of the situation from colleagues and the board, who wondered why they weren't focusing on the main job of the organisation: namely, that of growing and improving Bristol Pound's main operation. Increasingly, cracks and frustrations started to develop within the team.

BCU and Regulatory Restrictions

Looking back, whilst there is acknowledgement that, without BCU's regulatory role, it would have taken far longer to get the scheme off the ground, it is also clear with hindsight that the terms of the contract with BCU were not beneficial for the Bristol Pound.

For one thing, BCU had to control access to the data, because this was its responsibility in law. This meant that Bristol Pound had no idea who was paying whom, how much, and when. Without this information, it was not possible to intervene to resolve wrinkles, such as contacting businesses sitting on static balances to broker relationships with potential suppliers. It was also not possible to recognise and name businesses who were champions of the scheme. This would have been very useful in promoting the project and getting businesses to be excited about increasing their involvement.

The relationship with BCU also limited the kinds of experiments Bristol Pound could undertake. For example, there was the idea of trying out *demurrage*. In effect, this is like a negative interest rate, where your balance decreases if you don't spend the money in your account quickly. This might have helped encourage money to circulate more quickly. Equally, it might have discouraged businesses from accepting payment in the currency, of course. The point is, it would have been nice to be able to test out those hypotheses.

The clunkiness caused by having two accounting systems mirroring each other—Cyclos and the regulated BCU back-end—also counted heavily against the Bristol Pound. Topping up your account meant transferring money to the BCU account linked to your Bristol Pound account, but this would not be immediately visible on Cyclos because the mirroring didn't happen in real time. Instead, there was a daily batch update and reconciliation process, entailing a delay before you could access the money you'd just transferred. This lack of real time transactions meant that, as other instant payment apps came along, Bristol Pound stood no chance of meeting user expectations.

Finally, whilst numbers had been modelled as to the level of transactions needed to break even from transaction fees, a long-term plan for how to enable the currency to operate at that scale had not really been developed. Had it been, it would have been clear that BCU had neither the tech nor the levels of capital on their balance sheet required by regulation to enable it to operate at such a scale. BCU offered a quick fix, and not much thought was given to the longer term. This is understandable; getting something off the ground quickly was important. Scaling up would be a nice problem to have! But the way the agreements were framed with BCU, extracting the Bristol Pound from the relationship so that it could operate with a new partner and under a different regulation was always going to be a legal nightmare.

It is probably the case that not everyone on the board really understood the ramifications and downsides of going ahead with BCU. But those that did kept working on other options, in particular pursuing the goal of the Bristol Pound becoming regulated in its own right as a Small Electronic Money Institution (SEMI). This work took up significant amounts of time over the coming few years, but ultimately did not succeed. The reason was because the regulators themselves were under-resourced, and found themselves overwhelmed by a tsunami of ideas emerging from the fintech sector.

Mutual Credit

Mark and Ciaran were both committed to developing a mutual credit offer. Without this, there was no meaningful money creation, only a method for better circulating existing money. They had accepted that the Bristol Pound would launch first, but hoped that, in due course, the reputation of the Bristol Pound would build sufficient trust to make bringing in a mutual credit scheme easier. The network of Bristol Pound business members would create strong business relationships, such that they might well be prepared to extend credit to each other.

VALUE BEYOND MONEY

For Mark and Ciaran, the EU DigiPay money gave them hope that they could now devote some time and energy to developing the mutual credit side of things, under the brand name of Prospects. Soon after the funding was secured, Graham came back to the UK and was delighted to be offered the job of continuing his development of the Bristol Pound system, focusing this time on the more exciting work of developing the Prospects mutual credit operation. Steve headed up the job of reporting back to the EU, which involved various trips to Brussels. During one visit, he was delighted to find out that the Bristol Pound team were the poster boys for the entire funding stream.

Despite excitement on the part of many people on the team, Chris remembers this phase from a different perspective. The DigiPay money was serious EU money, with StrO as the lead partner for a consortium of several projects across Europe. Henk van Arkel, director of StrO, was the person with overall responsibility for the entire project. Chris saw the mutual credit project as Henk van Arkel's baby, with Ciaran and Steve trying to implement a version of it in Bristol. Meanwhile, EU project management processes are demanding, meaning Bristol Pound CIC had to rapidly professionalise. The organisation could suddenly employ several people, which was fantastic, but we urgently needed proper employment policies and procedures. We needed much stronger financial management too, which led to Bobbie coming on board as Finance Manager. The time was also right for a stronger board with more commercial experience.

Chris could see that, in reality, DigiPay funds would have to support the core Bristol Pound project as well as the mutual credit development. It was therefore no surprise to him that he soon saw tensions starting to emerge. At first, the tensions were between the board and those working on the mutual credit side of things. Later, they emerged between Bristol Pound CIC and StrO, as it became clear that the board was not as committed to implementing mutual credit as Henk had thought, potentially putting him in a difficult position with regard to his responsibility for the delivery of the DigiPay project.

Despite these emerging tensions, work on the mutual credit side progressed. Initially, there were questions to address about the level of separation between the main currency and the mutual credit project. On the one hand, the money in the Bristol Pound accounts could be a really useful capital pot of money to de-risk the mutual credit work. This, though, would have ramifications for the main Bristol Pound project, as the currency would no longer be 100% backed, potentially causing a lack of trust in the Bristol Pound itself. On the other hand, from the DigiPay funding perspective, the focus was all about non-sterling backed money creation, suggesting that there should be total separation between the Bristol Pound and the mutual credit scheme. The snag was that, with absolutely no risk money behind the mutual credit, it would likely be difficult to get businesses to commit to trying it out. At the end of the day, the deciding factor was the risk to the Bristol Pound organisation. What would happen to the currency if a major player in the credit clearing circle became insolvent and could not clear their liabilities to other members? In the end, Steve and the board were adamant that there would have to be a clear separation to safeguard the fully-backed Bristol Pound from the non-backed mutual credit scheme.

Communication with both businesses and the board was difficult. It was complicated to explain that bank money was created through debt, and that this method of funding investment was inherently linked to the boom-and-bust cycles that in turn impacted small businesses adversely. Businesses tended to trust their banks and to feel highly dependent on them. Most board members felt it was more important to do one thing well—the Bristol Pound—rather than risk that for the sake of something that most people couldn't even understand. The idea of staking the organisation's reputation on the ability of a group of small businesses to extend credit and repay each other, on the basis that it might theoretically improve the medium term or long term national economic outturn, was not feasible for most board members.

Graham, now back from Barcelona and delivering most of the technical work behind Prospects, began to get frustrated. He was investing much of his personal time in learning Cyclos, even becoming a volunteer for Qoin to increase his understanding of the system. He was excited to be doing this very innovative and potentially important work of creating an integrated platform for local currencies and mutual credit, but it was clear to him that the board was not really appreciative of his efforts. He started to get disillusioned, feeling that the big potential of the combined Bristol Pound and mutual credit operation was being lost.

James at the BCU was also involved in the DigiPay project. At first, like many on the team, he thought it was mainly about preparing to scale up the infrastructure of the Bristol Pound to cope with significant growth. He remembers meetings with Ciaran, who was talking about capturing 20% of the market in five years, with tens of millions of pounds passing through Bristol Pound operations annually. James felt these numbers were unrealistic. There were the "*Ciaranomics*" figures and the real figures, and no relationship between the two. But at one point, James remembers Henk from StrO coming over to discuss the project and suddenly realising that DigiPay was actually about mutual credit, which was something of a surprise to him. That said, James remembers getting involved in some interesting work, developing ideas about how the mutual credit side could integrate with their systems, and exploring fascinating concepts such as time-limited credits.

Steve was now full time, working in earnest on the rules of the Prospects scheme and talking to businesses about how they could see it working for them. The conversations didn't go as well as he'd hoped. Businesses were worried about what would happen if someone they'd given credit to went bust. This wasn't only a risk for the businesses; it was a real risk to the whole scheme. Such an event might well entail its instant demise, creating immediate losses for any business who had extended credit to another business. Try as he might, Steve could not create a set of rules that would avoid any risk of loss to businesses. Prospects would always rely on trust, on businesses acting honourably and responsibly.

Sighing, Ciaran tells me that he regrets that the DigiPay funding was not used to support the mutual credit work properly. In retrospect, he says he feels that if they'd taken the Bristol Pound project more slowly, and resolved the mutual credit arguments and approaches earlier on, the overall project could have had more impact. He wishes he'd somehow got the board to understand the importance and potential impact of mutual credit early on. Instead, he had tried to play a slowly, slowly, catchee monkey game to avoid arguments and build consensus. He says he took a slightly smoke and mirrors approach to explaining mutual credit, feeling that, without that, he would lose the support of the board entirely for this work.

Towards the end of the DigiPay project, there was a moment of existential crisis for the team. Another funding gap was looming, the currency scheme still needed lots of support to grow to a point where it was self-sustaining, and there was still no mutual credit solution in place. The team were searching for potential funders, and luckily came across P4NE. After an initial application, Steve, Graham and Ciaran were invited to Switzerland to pitch to their board: they would develop a ground-breaking and replicable local-currency-plus-mutual-credit system. P4NE were excited, and Bristol Pound CIC would be safe for another few years.

And yet, it proved even harder to deliver on the P4NE project. James was seconded to Manchester, which led to a gap in terms of BCU's involvement in this phase of development. But even without that blow, progress faltered on the mutual credit project. Steve felt, having by now talked to many potential business members, that Prospects would never get going in Bristol. Quite apart from the difficulty of explaining the scheme in ways that made sense to businesses, there were two issues. Firstly, businesses were not identifying a need for non-bank credit. Secondly, the necessary level of trust between businesses just wasn't there.

Steve was also developing franchise models to roll out the Bristol Pound solution to other cities. This side of the work was more successful. Exeter came on board and got fairly well established. Kingston upon Thames joined too. Other cities, including Cardiff and Edinburgh, were also talking to him about developing schemes.

Steve remembers a follow up presentation at P4NE to report on progress in June 2016. It was the eve of the historic referendum on whether Britain should leave the EU. P4NE were hosting a conference bringing together all the projects they were funding across Europe. Steve's presentation was well-received by the delegates and the P4NE board, and he felt proud to be a key player in a pan-European movement that could change the economic system. The future of the organisation seemed secure at last; there was now real potential to replicate our work not only in the UK but across Europe. But the dream was shattered on the train home, hearing the shocking news that his fellow citizens had voted for Brexit. The great pan-European movement would soon not include Bristol.

Beyond Bristol

In addition to the national work undertaken as part of the P4NE project, Graham worked up a successful bid to Innovate UK's first SBRI (Small Business Research Initiative) "Re-Imagining the High Street" funding round. This funding enabled Graham to work with the Totnes Pound on developing a digital solution for other local currencies so that they could operate at scale. A further aim was to build a system that would also enable local currencies to transfer funds between each other, creating a joined-up network of

VALUE BEYOND MONEY

currencies across the nation. Sadly, Bristol Pound was not successful in the larger, second round of funding. Graham was interested to see what did win, but when he found out he was disappointed. He describes the winning project as a surveillance capitalism scheme, using personal data to drive economic growth, completely out of line with what the Bristol Pound was trying to achieve.

Graham was also successful in an application to Joseph Rowntree Foundation to develop a community of practice for local currencies. At first this was called the Guild of Independent Currencies (GOIC), and, with a later funding pot, morphed to become the Independent Money Alliance (IMA). This funding enabled Bristol Pound to run several conferences, which were attended by academics and activists from across the country and Europe. A group from Barcelona came to one event, and the team took some credit from seeing how their ideas helped to shape the development of Barcelona's own local currency, the REC (Real Economy Currency).

Sarah Forrester remembers travelling to events in Europe. These gatherings provided an opportunity to share learning with delegates representing various currencies from around the world. Indeed, it was in Nantes, France that she met people from the Brazilian Palmas currency, a meeting that in the longer term resulted in Sarah moving to Brazil, where she continues to design systemic interventions across a wide variety of sectors.

But despite the success of this outreach work, there were some tensions emerging between Graham and the management team. Graham remembers one conference in Liverpool that office staff had not been invited to attend because of the pressure of work. Graham felt that attending conferences should be prioritised. One member of staff had gone as far as to pay for her own ticket and attend in her own time because she was so keen to be there. At the conference, Graham could see that other local currencies had brought all their staff along. A little while later, there was a similar event in Brixton. Graham decided to use his budget to take all the office staff to London, without telling Ciaran or Steve. On finding no staff in the office that day, there was understandable frustration that internal communications and shared decision-making processes had fallen apart so drastically.

Stresses

At the start, things were so positive. While there were slight differences in the motivations people had around why they wanted to create a local currency, the shared aim of getting this innovative new project off the ground really brought everyone together. People were working autonomously on different aspects of the project, and when they came together to collaborate, there was mutual trust and celebration of the strides that were being taken.

But at some point, around a year on from the launch, that started to change. Once the initial excitement subsided, the reality of the on-going effort to make the scheme function well became more apparent. Sorting out glitches and customer issues were less rewarding tasks than the initial ideation and creation phase. Money came to the project, meaning that people were being paid for work that for most had been completely voluntary up to that point, and new people joined the team. But the formalisation that came particularly with the EU funding created more hierarchy and distance between staff, managers, and board members, many of whom were not steeped in the philosophical arguments that had been the subject of all the early conversations between the founders. Additionally, the many pots of money being brought in were to fund various exciting projects, but crucially not the day job of delivering and growing the Bristol Pound, which was the board's main goal. This led to many feeling unappreciated for the effort they were putting in on the funded work, whilst the board were increasingly frustrated with the seeming distractions from what they saw as the main job of the organisation.

Ciaran pauses as he considers how the energy changed, then offers: *"The initial excitement blinded people to the reality of where we would end up."* The kinds of issues that emerged a year after launch are common to many startups, whether commercial or non-profit. Success creates emergent problems and day to day challenges that need resolving. Suddenly, there are customer complaints to be handled, software bugs to be fixed, difficult choices to be made about how the limited funds should be spent, deadlines for reports to funders to be met, and performance issues to be addressed.

And of course, life was carrying on for everyone on the team. Ciaran became a father twice over, once in 2013 and again in 2018. Funding came and went and people had to flex their hours accordingly, and find other work to fill the gaps in their income. People went travelling and responded to major life events. Bristol Pound couldn't be everyone's top priority all of the time.

Staff Management

Steve gives a good insight into the staff management problems. The initial group of five founders had become close friends who enjoyed working together. All had strong personalities with clear visions that they communicated vociferously. When the organisation grew quickly after the DigiPay funding, although an induction process had been put in place, it was difficult for staff and volunteers joining the team to really get under the skin of the organisation. The new team members were bright and full of ideas, but they largely had to learn on the job and were not involved enough in decision making.

Staff learned experientially what was and wasn't working, and in some cases had very relevant operational experience. But the organisation had become hierarchical, with insufficient opportunities for the executive team to learn from those below. Staff sometimes found themselves in the difficult position of trying to deliver things that they knew were not deliverable. This was demoralising as they felt they were seen as not performing effectively.

A compounding factor was the lack of employee management training amongst most of those tasked with managing the staff team, and the lack of a dedicated HR function within the organisation. This made recruitment, induction, and ongoing staff management rather haphazard.

Initially, Ciaran had been directly managing all staff members as CEO. However, with the team growing, this structure was no longer working. So, at some point in 2014, Mark took over the line management of the staff team. He enjoyed the challenge, and was seen as doing well. Mark felt his role was to shield the staff from the rapidly changing high level priority list that was causing them so much stress, and to support the team to deliver in a more structured way. Mark reported to Ciaran and the board, and for a while all went well.

However, Mark could see that he was oiling a machine that wasn't really working. He recalls: *"We were spending a lot of money paying staff to grow usage of the currency—it was a very inefficient use of funds."* He wasn't convinced by the organisation's direction of travel, so, after some hard thought, he decided to leave. In retrospect, he wonders if he was too quick to call time on his involvement; perhaps he could have intervened more to change the direction. But at the time, he felt that if growth was what was wanted, then Mike would be a better person to manage the team to deliver this. Recognising Mike's skills in forming relationships with businesses, and acknowledging the fact that Mike was local and well connected—important attributes for growing a local membership—Mark felt that stepping down was the best thing he could do for the organisation. He was also aware that the Plough and Share Credit Union, more local to him, needed his support and energy. And so in spring 2015 he moved on, with Mike picking up the management reins.

Unlike many members of the staff team, Mike was highly goal oriented and, he tells me, "relentlessly driven". He thinks this was probably why he was promoted to being the manager of the staff team. But he didn't really feel he had the necessary leadership credentials. For a start, he felt spread very thin. As well as working flat out for the Bristol Pound, he was trying to do a PhD. Furthermore, he felt there was a lack of infrastructure to support him in a management role. As a small organisation, there was very little formality in terms of job descriptions and objective-setting. It would be down to him to develop and impose working practices and targets if he were to get the team to deliver what was needed.

Mike started to look at the financial model, to work out what the targets needed to be for his team. What he discovered was a bombshell: to break even, for every business recruited (and thus subject to an onboarding fee from BCU), at least £500 needed to be transacted through the Cyclos system. Only then would Bristol Pound's transaction charges create sufficient income to cover the onboarding fee. Mike suddenly realised that all the work he'd been doing recruiting businesses was actually incurring a deficit; he was just handing over money to BCU.

When Mike had first joined the organisation, he had felt very supported by Ciaran. Ciaran mentored him and helped him develop his pitching skills. But by the time Mike started to manage the team, he felt Ciaran had little spare capacity for providing him with direction or support. As Mike started to learn more about the finances through his new management role, he came to understand why there was so much tension between the executive team and the staff: the organisation's funding was to deliver Prospects, not the Bristol Pound. The staff team he was managing just wanted to build the Bristol Pound, and they were frustrated that the executive team seemed so absent from that vision.

Meanwhile, the day-to-day challenges were immense. Katie left in the summer of 2015, and there was a period of three months with nobody doing communications and marketing. There was the challenge of the new series of notes to launch, and the complex process of trying to exchange all the old

VALUE BEYOND MONEY

notes that people and businesses were holding for the new notes before they expired. This was something that Jen Green remembers well, as she had to coordinate and keep records of the process. There was a joint campaign with Good Energy which had the potential to create a new income stream, but created lots of extra work. The many side projects, such as Real Economy, GOIC, the launch of the Exeter Pound, presentations for people from all over the world—all these things spread Mike ever thinner, making him even less able to deliver on the main job of supporting his team to grow the Bristol Pound. Feeling overwhelmed, Mike eventually suffered burnout, and he left the organisation in late 2015.

2015 Bristol Pound Notes. Above: Fronts. Below: Backs.

Various people had a go at managing the staff team in 2016—including, for a short while, Graham. He tells me that the pattern of firefighting and constantly changing priorities continued, and that he too felt he had no consistent direction or support. That said, he felt empowered by having a budget to manage, so he just got on with what he thought was important using that money as he saw fit. But after a few months, convinced that the executive team and the board didn't understand his approach and aware that he, too, was spread far too thin, he stepped down as the manager of the staff team. Anna Bryher took over. Graham went back to focusing on the IMA and on working with developers. At this point, work was starting on the creation of a Bristol Pound payment app, which would provide a much-needed improvement to the user experience, with text-to-pay by that stage seeming very antiquated compared to the likes of ApplePay.

Leadership Problems

When the P4NE funding was secured, Ciaran tells me he started to feel hopeful again. He knew what was needed was a common aim to pull the staff and directors back together, and he felt the P4NE project could provide that. With frustration showing in his voice, he says, "*I thought, 'this is it—we're being paid to do these things.'*" But somehow the board, which by this time was much larger and included several newer members from the wider community, didn't seem to share the aims of the P4NE funding. In effect, they were wedded to a vision that was not in line with what the organisation was being paid to do. Ciaran explains sadly: "*We wanted [the project] to belong to the community, but the community didn't really understand it.*" The people on the board representing the arts and the community were not very engaged in the business or economic aspects of the project, whilst the people on the business side were highly pragmatic, focusing on key performance indicators (KPIs) specific to the Bristol Pound currency. The board was not keen to shift their vision and embrace new economic ideas like non-bank credit creation. Ciaran berates himself for not having educated the board more about the underlying economic arguments that went way beyond printing pretty money to encourage people to shop at independent stores. From his perspective, the board was made up of a group of people who loved the idea of a quirky local currency, but who lacked the technical knowledge about what they were trying to achieve in economic terms. He had hoped James at BCU would bring that expertise as a partner, but in reality BCU had their own goals in mind when they decided to get involved with the project.

Most of the rest of the board had a different perspective. They felt frustrated that time was being wasted on Prospects, when to them it was obvious that it wasn't going to work. Meanwhile, they saw the main task of nurturing the Bristol Pound currency as suffering from a lack of management support and direction.

Looking back, Ciaran says wistfully that if the organisation had prioritised creating a mutual credit system, they could have taken a very different approach. They could have launched without regulation, just as a voluntary agreement between businesses. They could have started very small and grown organically and iteratively, building on the learning they developed. They could have worked towards achieving

SEMI regulation once they reached the kinds of thresholds that would have made that necessary. At the end of the day, it's impossible to say whether such an approach would have worked any better. But regardless, history cannot be rewritten, and this was not the approach that was taken.

Graham remembers feelings of disillusionment coming to a head for him soon after the EU referendum, when he was giving a talk in Glasgow. It was clear to him that the entire Bristol Pound spiel no longer resonated. The country was now in a new place and artistic paper notes were not the answer. What was needed was a new offer that could create impact in socio-economic terms by boosting the real economy (that is, production and trade of goods and services) and supporting local economies in the post-Brexit era. Much of the language Bristol Pound was using had been honed when the organisation was delivering the EU funded project, with a vision of European collaboration on a new economic model.

From Graham's perspective, the newer board members were not radical activists, keen to experiment and envision new approaches from the ground up. Rather, they were top-down leaders, imposing a business model and direction that were not fit for the emerging reality of a new post-Brexit economy. For him, the vision should have been about developing new economic interventions. For the board, the vision was to grow the Bristol Pound. Graham saw himself as focused outwardly, looking at changes in the movement across Europe and the world, and identifying opportunities to develop something new and impactful. He saw the board as focused inwardly, on banging its own drum. Meanwhile, the board saw Graham as putting his efforts in the wrong places.

VALUE BEYOND MONEY

Graham says his disappointment peaked when representatives from the Chiemgauer currency—operating in the Chiemgau Alps in Southern Germany—came to visit. He had been liaising with them for years and was desperate to meet with them in person, to spend quality time with like-minded people, developing ideas for what needed to come next in the world of local currencies. But he was not included in the visit, and there was no opportunity for him to have those groundbreaking conversations. He feels that the board missed a huge opportunity because they didn't understand the importance of having a big discussion about how to power up local currencies to deliver something that would have real impact.

Chris was also struggling somewhat with the leadership of the board at this time. He was chair, but also finance director, putting him in the awkward position of having to try to be inclusive and fair in strategic decisions, but also tough on financial decisions. He was trying to hold the organisation together and keep it safe when he felt it was pulling apart at the seams. He describes his role as a goalkeeper, constantly leaping to save the ball. Meanwhile, the Real Economy, which he had founded as a project within Bristol Pound, had split off to become an independent entity, and at the end of 2016 he felt the time was right to move on and concentrate on that instead.

I need to introduce Ben Heald at this point. Ben had joined the board in November 2015. A serial entrepreneur, he was at that time heading up Sift, a digital design and publishing company that he had founded some years earlier. Amongst other things, he was also a trustee of the concert hall St George's Bristol. Ben had come across the Bristol Pound soon after it launched in 2012 and was immediately taken with the idea. Ben says: "*The idea of a city trying to take control of its destiny using a money platform is interesting, and the things you could do with it are amazing.*" He started giving out Bristol Pounds to members of his staff team to celebrate significant achievements. When he saw an advert requesting that people put themselves forward to be a business representative on the board, he jumped at the opportunity to be involved.

At first, Ben took somewhat of a back seat. He was assuming his main role would be to help on the marketing challenge, which played to his strengths. Ciaran, Steve and Bobbie seemed to be running things, and there was plenty of funding coming in. But gradually Ben became aware that the board wasn't functioning as well as he'd thought. The staff team seemed to be dissatisfied, and there was a lack of challenge around what people were actually spending their time doing. He started to think he could bring value to the organisation thanks to his leadership skills, and when Chris stood down as chair, Ben stepped up. It was September 2016.

Ben tried to restore peace. He reviewed the position of CEO, a post held by Ciaran up to that point, thinking a change of leadership might help. But nobody else seemed keen to challenge Ciaran for a variety of reasons, so he continued in the role.

By the start of 2017, Sarah, Mark, Katie, Mike, and most recently Chris, had already left the organisation. Of the founding team, David remained as a non-executive director, and Ciaran and Steve were executive directors. Ben remembers there were still a lot of positivity around the GOIC and IMA meetings, and enthusiasm from committed business members. But the disagreement over Prospects was pulling the organisation apart. Ben's view was that the organisation should just tell P4NE that we were not able to deliver Prospects, and hope that they would let us keep the funding to work on the job of growing the Bristol Pound and spreading the approach to other cities. However, the founders remained wedded to the idea of making Prospects work for too long, from Ben's perspective. When eventually the decision to give up on Prospects was agreed, there was a resulting ripple through the organisation, hastening the forthcoming change in its executive leadership. But for Ben, by this stage a great deal of momentum had been lost on the development of the Bristol Pound.

At this point, there were three executive directors: Steve, Ciaran, and Graham (though Bobbie was soon to become a director, having already been part of the executive team since her appointment as Finance Manager). All three were white and male. All three were passionate workaholics and had strong and sometimes competing ideas of where the organisation should be focusing its efforts. There were several disagreements and clashes. Some people I've talked to have said that the atmosphere was testosterone-heavy, others that there were macho attitudes to things like work-life balance and burnout that were unhelpful, and that in fact led to the very burnout they were trying to suppress.

It's worth commenting on the lack of diversity in the founding team. Getting the project off the ground required several things of its founders. It required significant amounts of unpaid time—something you were only likely to be able to do if you had sufficient financial resources not to have to prioritise paid work. Alternatively, it required that you were already educated to degree level and were willing and able to give up work to focus on your post graduate education, and make the project the focus of your study. It required sufficient knowledge of economics that you could both critique the status quo and envisage new approaches. It required a level of self-belief and confidence that challenging the status quo was even possible. Taken together, it's not surprising that the founders and early executive directors fit a fairly narrow mould.

Despite this superficial lack of diversity, many of the people I interviewed commented that the wider team felt very diverse. There were several women on the staff and volunteer team, and some female directors too. The team encompassed people from their early twenties through to middle age, and brought together those from a wide range of backgrounds and with radically different world outlooks: a priest, an activist, lawyers, scientists, entrepreneurs. In the early days at least, the team not only worked hard together, it played hard together too, with pub evenings after work that always involved deep and challenging conversations about life, the universe and everything.

It would be fair to say that the ethnic diversity of the team did not fully reflect Bristol's wider community. Whilst that is not ideal, it is perhaps unfair to single Bristol Pound out on this. The voluntary sector in the UK generally has an issue in creating organisations that represent the make-up of our society. According to Civil Society[14], in 2021, 9.5% of workers in the charity sector were from a minority ethnic background, some way short of the 13.1% representation in society.

During the first few months of 2017, tensions in the executive team continued to build. Graham was finding his

---

14   www.civilsociety.co.uk

role increasingly frustrating, and his health suffered as a result. With law exams on the horizon, he decided to leave in the spring of 2017.

All Change

By this point, the organisation was in real trouble. The staff team was suffering from a lack of management and direction. Steve and Ciaran felt they were doing their best to support the core Bristol Pound project, but were still having to spend large amounts of their time on other funded work, like trying to deliver on the P4NE outcomes, pursuing becoming a SEMI, and attempting to develop technology to enable card payments from Bristol Pound accounts. Ben realised he needed a stronger board if he were to have any hope of driving through the sorts of changes that he felt were needed to save the organisation and the currency. He went about recruiting new board members urgently.

The refreshed board encouraged the executive team to refocus on growing the Bristol Pound currency usage, resulting in a new surge of energy that summer. But it was too little, too late. Usage of the currency had been declining for a year already by this stage.

Over the coming months, the funding began to dry up and the entire staff team left. To be clear, not everyone left because of burnout or stress. Undoubtedly, other life events were also occurring in people's lives that meant they needed to move on. Still, it was a time of great challenge for the organisation and of major decisions for Ben. As chair, he felt his main role was to support the CEO, but with all the staff leaving it was clear that a change was needed. Being an entrepreneur himself, Ben had a lot of compassion for where the founders now found themselves. Ben explains that founders have a vision and huge passion for their work. They put in immense effort for little reward for years. But then reality kicks in. Sticking doggedly to the original vision doesn't always work. Flexibility and pragmatism are needed, but founders are often overly aligned to their original vision. Meanwhile, the qualities and skills required to found an organisation—the ability to spot a problem and an opportunity, and the technical knowledge to develop a solution—are perhaps not the same qualities and skills needed to develop and sustain a venture through the vicissitudes of life.

By late 2017, Ben felt he had a board that would support him in the challenging process of restructuring the executive team. Difficult decisions were taken in the spring 2018. That summer, Ciaran left the organisation completely, whilst Steve left his executive role but remained on the board as a non-executive director. David was the only other board member who had been there from the outset. And I was hired as the new managing director, with no inkling of the journey that had got the organisation to that point. I had a few meetings with Ciaran and Steve in my first week or so, and then was on my own in terms of picking up the day-to-day management of the organisation.

CHAPTER FOUR
A LOOK UNDER THE BONNET

*In which we discover some of the
realities of running a local currency*

This chapter will focus on the nuts and bolts of what I discovered about how the Bristol Pound currency operated when I joined.

As already discussed, the broad goal of the currency was to encourage localisation, both to reduce the transport-related use of oil and to build a more resilient and prosperous local economy. The focus of the operation was therefore very much on local businesses, helping them to attract more local shoppers and to encourage them to use local suppliers.

Bar a few exceptions that have already been mentioned, only businesses that met tight membership criteria could set up a Bristol Pound account, which was needed to interact with digital money. These criteria basically ensured that members were independent, rather than a subsidiary of a larger business, and based locally, evidenced by having a BS postcode. And there was some leniency. For example, farms just outside the BS postcode area who were supplying food to the city could still be members. As already mentioned, First Bus, which operated (and continues to operate) most of the buses in the city, was also welcomed. In part this was because there was a feeling that ideally people should be able to choose to live wholly within the currency; that is, for it to be a fully-fledged alternative currency, rather than just a complementary one. Enabling people to live fully within the currency system entailed enabling payments for basic services like public transport as well as for local taxes.

Business members could choose whether to accept only paper Bristol Pounds, only digital Bristol Pounds, or both. In reality, as a team, we had very little ability to police this. For example, there were reports of a Tesco supermarket accepting the paper Bristol Pounds. Whilst this was somewhat at odds with the aims of the currency, at least we could be sure that those pounds would be re-spent in Bristol, so there was little need to get upset about it. The key thing was that Tesco could not be a member, and could not therefore benefit from the publicity we were putting out on behalf of our business members. There were also reports that a drug dealer was accepting Bristol Pounds. Even though this was a reputational risk to the organisation, there was really nothing we could do to stop paper money circulating to support any economic activity that people using the currency were engaging in.

A bigger problem was that many of the businesses who joined on the basis that they would benefit from the marketing did not, in reality, accept Bristol Pounds in payment. We would get complaints from people saying that they had gone to a particular shop or café listed in the directory or on the app, tried to pay in Bristol Pounds, and were told they couldn't. We would contact the businesses to find out what was going wrong. Sometimes they were apologetic and blamed it on staff training problems. Other times it was clear from their responses that they were basically free-riding; benefiting from our promotional work despite not actually following through and accepting the currency. For many, taking Bristol Pounds in payment was seen as too much of a hassle.

But once they were in the network and had opened a digital account, we had no power to force them to close it, and so they were shown on our online and printed directories. Even if they hadn't opened a digital account, if they told us they were accepting the paper money and we had printed their name in a directory, that directory was going to be in circulation for a year or two, and we couldn't take that marketing away from them. The inability of people to spend their Bristol Pounds consistently with businesses listed as members was meanwhile one of the reasons that some individuals gave for desisting with the currency.

Of course, there were individual members too. You didn't need to become an individual member to buy the paper currency, but you had to if you wanted to open an account for the digital money. To be a member of the currency scheme, you either had to reside in the BS postcode area, work in it, or be a student in Bristol. Fairly quickly, and increasingly after the launch of the payment app in 2018, the digital currency operations outstripped the paper operations. By the end of 2018, only about 10% of the total transactions were in the paper currency. The notes were mainly popular with tourists, and the most prolific issuer of paper currency for many years was the Tourist Information Centre, which, like the Bristol Pound itself, now no longer exists.

In reality, the paper money and the digital money were two

completely different products, governed by different rules and managed in completely different ways.

Paper Bristol Pounds

The first thing to make clear is that paper Bristol Pounds were not legal tender. They were not bank notes. In England and Wales, only the Bank of England has the right to issue bank notes, and those notes are the only legal tender. The only things that local currency schemes can issue that function like money are pre-purchased vouchers with an expiry date. These fall outside FCA regulations, simplifying administration and red tape significantly.

To safeguard people's money should the scheme end, all the money used to buy paper Bristol Pounds was put into a trust account held at BCU. Various businesses around the city, as well as BCU itself, operated exchange services for us, as already mentioned. Anyone could go into one of our Cash Points and buy paper Bristol Pounds with sterling. Some businesses even accepted card payments for Bristol Pounds.

Behind the scenes, we were running around with bundles of paper Bristol Pounds to top up the Cash Points to an agreed float, maintaining records of sales of Bristol Pounds at each Cash Point, collecting in the sterling received in exchange for the paper Bristol Pounds, banking the sterling, and finally reconciling the balances of all the Cash Points, safes, and the trust account itself (using a very complex spreadsheet, affectionately known, when I joined, as "the monster"). This all added up to be about a three-day-a week job.

Meanwhile, the businesses were administering the Cash

VALUE BEYOND MONEY

Points out of good will. Of course, mistakes happened; Cash Point floats would accidentally get mixed with takings in the till, for example, and agreeing resolutions to such problems was a further drain on both Bristol Pound and on the Cash Point operators. Record keeping was generally poor, as it often is with cash transactions, and it was impossible to prove exactly what had caused the errors. Several thousand pounds' worth of such errors were written off over the years, and relationships with the Cash Point businesses, who were helping us out for no financial reward, could be strained.

As the paper Bristol Pounds were classified as vouchers, each one had to show an expiry date. This was often misunderstood by people, who either didn't notice the expiry date, or who thought we had put an expiry date in the small print to defraud them in some way. At the point of writing this book, I still get contacted occasionally by people with out-of-date vouchers, hoping that we will reimburse them in sterling. We just can't. We have no funds to do that, and indeed the CIC has now wound up. I did make the odd exception when we were still operating, like that time a child contacted me who had cracked open their piggy bank and found an expired £B20 note in it.

Over the course of the nine years of operations, three editions of notes were produced, each with a three-year expiry date. A separate trust account was set up for each edition of notes. When an edition of notes was due to expire, the team ran campaigns to encourage people to swap their old notes for new notes, to ensure they could still spend them. However, on each occasion, many notes were effectively lost. These were sometimes notes that tourists had bought and taken home to stick on their fridges. In other cases, they were gifts that had not been spent, with the recipient perhaps not understanding the scheme and expiry date problem. And life happens, right? Some notes just disappeared down the backs of sofas or went through washing machines by accident. There was therefore an amount of money left in the trust account a few months after the expiry of the notes, and that money was then taken as "seigniorage" income by Bristol Pound CIC. In 2018, the expiry of the 2015 notes provided just over £75,000 of income.

The paper Bristol Pounds were the most visible aspect of the Bristol Pound scheme, and for this reason they were seen as very important to the currency's success. But as already discussed, for each edition, there was a public competition to organise for the artwork, an exhibition to host, and a voting process to be facilitated. The notes then had to be designed and printed to a high quality, with expensive anti-fraud features such as holograms and watermarks. The costs associated with the production of the paper currency, plus the staffing costs of administering it described above, plus the losses that were incurred through errors—these all added up to a significant amount. It's hard to be precise because detailed records from the early days no longer exist, but it is fair to say that despite the seigniorage income, the paper currency operations did not break even.

Digital Bristol Pounds

The digital money was a completely different kettle of fish. Operating digital money, especially on behalf of consumers, is, by contrast with paper vouchers, heavily regulated. As already mentioned, Cyclos had been identified as an ideal user interface for the digital currency, but was not regulated. As a result, we'd had to partner with Bristol Credit Union. Like the Bristol Pound, BCU was focused on offering services that were beneficial for Bristol's communities, providing an alternative to profit-focused mainstream financial service providers, so they seemed ideal. This solution worked from a regulatory and technical perspective, but as you will remember from the last chapter, it was clunky.

Each time someone wanted to open a digital Bristol Pound account, they were basically going through two parallel administrative processes: one for them to join the Bristol Pound, and the other for them to create an account at the credit union. This latter process was quite involved, as it had to cover formal "know your customer" protocols (to avoid the potential for fraud and money laundering) required by the regulatory framework within which BCU operated. Assuming applicants got through those processes (and when I joined in 2018, only about one in ten applicants got as far as successfully creating an account), they then needed to be helped to use all the systems, including the online Cyclos interface, BCU's back-end interface (if they wanted to extract money back to sterling or get financial statements), and the SMS interface for paying by phone. The number of emails people got from ourselves and BCU in the first week of signing up was enough to put off all but the most committed.

Then of course there was the fact that, as mentioned, this was not a real time interface. If you put money into the BCU account linked to your Bristol Pound account on Cyclos, it wouldn't immediately be on the Cyclos system for you to spend. The batch update process that kept the BCU system in sync with Cyclos ran each afternoon and had a cut off time for transactions that would be processed. The update took quite some time, meaning it could take over a day for funds you'd transferred to appear on your Cyclos account, ready for you to spend.

Text-to-pay was also extremely unwieldy. First, the user had to be able to send the message such that the automated system could interpret it. The messages went something like this: "Pay 1234 BristolBooks 5.95". The first number was your individual number (PIN), "BristolBooks" was the short name of the business, which had to be written precisely, and the last element of the message was the amount. There was a great deal of scope for getting messages wrong in some minor way. More than that, for each message to get through, the user had to have coverage from their phone network. The message would then be picked up in Cyclos, a process which sometimes failed. Then Cyclos would send a confirmation message to both parties, using some third-party tech that occasionally didn't work. For those messages to be received, both the customer's and the trader's phone needed to have network coverage too. Needless to say, there were often problems with SMS messages not getting through, or getting delayed so that people would assume a payment hadn't been successful and therefore pay again, only for both transactions to be processed. Let's just say that quick and frictionless payment was not something we could offer and much time was wasted on the part of individual members, business members, and Bristol Pound staff in sorting out text-to-pay problems.

We did what we could to bring our tech up to date. First, we tried to implement payment cards. Initially it looked promising. A solution was trialled and seemed to be working. We bought thousands of plastic cards, along with a machine to personalise them, and everyone got very excited. However, as the testing continued, it became clear that the system didn't actually work effectively after all, and the plans had to be dropped. I only discovered this failed project when I came across all the cards in 2019, packing up to move offices.

Apple launched ApplePay in 2014, and within a few short years, paying using a smartphone was normal. In response, we worked with Scott Logic to develop a payment app, which we launched in 2018. This included a map and directory of businesses and cash exchange points. You could walk around the city, see what Bristol Pound businesses were nearby, click on the business you'd just walked into, and pay. These were "push" payments: you keyed in the amount on your phone rather than the shop initiating the transaction, and then showed your phone to the person behind the till so that they could see confirmation that the payment had gone through. This was soon seen as much more reliable and significantly faster than the old text-to-pay method. However, it was still far from perfect, especially from the trader's perspective, as they had no control over the payment, nor did they have confirmation that the transaction had been successful apart from via the customer's phone.

In 2019, Nic Hemley, director and Chief Technical Officer for my first year or so in post, and Owen Davis, who had previously worked on graphic design for us back in the early days, developed a significant upgrade to the app. This enabled the "know your customer" element of onboarding new users to happen seamlessly within the app itself. The driver for this significant investment was to improve on the awful statistic that only one in ten people starting the application process actually persevered to the point of opening an account, and from that perspective the upgrade was a great success. But the payments were still push payments, making payments far slower at the till than for someone using ApplePay.

In 2019, we were still getting complaints about text-to-pay not working. It wasn't a surprise to us because we knew just how unreliable it was. We wanted to just stop offering this payment option because there was no way of improving mobile phone coverage or the performance of third-party tech. But there were many stalwarts of text-to-pay who insisted on using it; they were some of our longest standing and most loyal users. They didn't want to get an app. They didn't want to get a smartphone. They were concerned about their personal data being harvested by the mobile phone provider and by any apps they might use on it. I understood and shared their worries, though I personally had taken the easier route of sighing and reluctantly using smartphones and apps to fit in with the expectations of friends, family, work and businesses. Part of me applauded their ethically-driven stubborn adherence to text-to-pay, but from an operational perspective, it was very frustrating.

My favourite complaint deserves a paragraph all to itself. Someone contacted me in 2019 to say that they were in an independent store and saw the £B sticker at the till. They were in a slow queue waiting to be served. So they thought, "I know, I'll download the app, turn some money into Bristol Pounds, and I'll be able to pay in Bristol Pounds at the till. Cool!" The assumption was that this would take maybe 5 or 10 minutes, based on their experience of other phone payment apps. I had to reply recognising their frustration, sadly explaining the reality was that it was more likely to take 5 to 10 days to achieve what they thought they could accomplish in a similar number of minutes. It was my wake-up call that we were nowhere near able to meet user expectations, even with our new and improved app.

From a business model perspective, the digital money worked far less well than the paper operations. Every month there was an invoice from BCU for the administrative costs of setting up new users, etc. There was then a corresponding statement covering the transaction costs paid by merchants, and this represented the income to us. Then there was a balance to be settled. I never once saw a month in which the balance was payable to us. BCU's administrative costs of providing the regulated back-end outstripped the transaction fee income every month. It's worth saying that despite this, BCU's costs of providing these services to Bristol Pound CIC were far from covered.

There was no way we could put up transaction fees. In 2018, they were already greater than many businesses were having to pay for other sorts of digital payments services. But the payment to BCU each month represented only a tiny fraction of the costs for running the digital money infrastructure. There were also expenses involved in developing and maintaining the Cyclos interface, developing and hosting the app, and so on. To break even and cover the wider running costs of the organisation, we would have needed payments to grow by a factor of at least 50. I talked to James about our need to radically change our marketing to enable that kind of growth, but was told that if the currency grew by a factor of 50, they wouldn't be able to offer the service at all. I'll come back to the detail of why in a little while.

Localisation - The Reality

There is one more concern that I became aware of as I appraised the functioning of the currency and its aims of localisation when I joined. I wasn't alone in having this concern, and from conversations, I suspect it was one of the reasons that some people didn't join up.

If I drink coffee, eat chocolate (or avocados, or mangos), use smartphones and computers, or buy the most ethical all-rubber wellington boots. I must understand that these goods rely on global trade. We don't grow coffee in Bristol. Similarly, our beloved IT products rely on semiconductors, which are produced overwhelmingly in Taiwan, South Korea, Japan, the USA and China. In terms of reducing transport-related CO_2 emissions, it makes little difference who my immediate supplier is. At some point in the supply chain, goods are being transported thousands of miles to enable my purchase.

You might say that at least buying these products from local independent businesses means that the community wealth building goal of a localised currency is met. But is that such a good thing? Surely if I really want to be ethical, I should be cutting out the middle-person and ensuring I have as direct a route as possible to the originator of the product. That way, the trade is fairer, with the farmers and workers getting a higher proportion of the money I'm paying, instead of various intermediaries all taking their cut along the way.

VALUE BEYOND MONEY

The lack of clarity and obfuscation enabled by having long supply chains also means I'm far less likely to know what the production methods or conditions for workers are like. To make a well-informed decision about what to buy, I need to have as much information about the producer as I can, and that requires as direct a relationship as possible.

The brand I'm buying is also key in all this. If I buy Coca Cola from a local independent shop, I'm still supporting Coca Cola. I don't want to single out Coca Cola; the same goes for all food and beverages produced and marketed by large multinational companies. Their general aim is to create highly addictive products that—it is now clear from lots of different research—are mostly bad for human health, quite apart from any negative environmental or profiteering effects they may have. A currency aiming to localise trade doesn't make my choice of buying Coca Cola any more ethical. If we think ultra-processed foods and sugar or aspartame-filled drinks are generally a bad thing, we have to not buy them, period. It makes no difference to Coca Cola whether we buy them at McDonalds, at Tesco's, or at a locally-owned grocery store; all purchases add to their bottom line. But if we all stopped buying Coca Cola tomorrow... Now, that would have an impact.

CHAPTER FIVE
COULD I SAVE THE BRISTOL POUND?

In which we discover that operating a local currency is not as easy as we might think

So, here I was in my new job. The new 2018 notes had been launched just a few days before I started and there was much excitement in the office. But within the first week, I discovered that the Bristol Pound was in crisis. With current operational costs, there was about six months' worth of money left. Usage of the currency was declining and had been for a couple of years. I realised then that the reason I'd been hired was because I had a track record in helping ailing non-profit organisations get back on their feet. My job was to save the Bristol Pound.

2018 Bristol Pound Notes - Fronts

VALUE BEYOND MONEY

2018 Bristol Pound Notes - Backs

I started to uncover some of the problems that were holding us back. There was the tech issue that I've already outlined, but that was just too expensive to tackle until we had significant funding coming in. And before we could convince anyone to fund us, we needed to have popular support and to be seen as meeting a demand from our users. However, we had falling usage and business members leaving, which was the complete opposite of the story I needed to be telling potential funders. The questions I needed to answer were: why couldn't we attract new users, and why were businesses leaving?

What Would Make Businesses Want To Join?

In the first few weeks of being in post, I met Martin Parker, author of "Shut Down the Business School". Despite his book title, he had just landed a post in the School of Management at the University of Bristol, and he told me that he was interested in alternative economy experiments aimed at diversifying the local economy. He had access to funding for research and wondered if there were useful questions that some academic research might answer. We soon settled on the need to understand what businesses required from the Bristol Pound. If we were to survive, we needed to reverse the exodus of business members. Thomas Sealy, a researcher within Martin's team, undertook the research in early 2019, talking to a variety of small businesses—some members, some not. He asked what benefits the Bristol Pound currently brought, and what would make membership more useful. He also asked what things small businesses were struggling with.

The answers to the research questions made our situation very clear: the Bristol Pound itself did very little for businesses. Indeed, for most members, the currency was just an extra hassle that they could do without.

This was not news to me. In my short time with the organisation, I'd already had several uncomfortable conversations with business members and ex-business members. For businesses, there were several problems in being part of the currency. For starters, there were the many Bristol Pound payment methods, all of which required extra training for their front-of-house staff. If you ran a coffee shop, you might have a new staff member every month. There's lots to train new starters on. There are the basics, of course; about food hygiene, how to use the coffee machine, how to operate the till for cash and card payments. And then there's the specific Bristol Pound training; how to recognise and check the validity of the paper Bristol Pounds, how to process text-to-pay and Bristol Pound app payments. On top of that, there is how to ensure the digital payments have gone through, with the text-to-pay system being totally different from the app. Different buttons on the till need to be pressed for each payment method—which all have to be set up in advance, of course—so that the till could be reconciled. If the business had more than one till, the member of staff would also have to write each text-to-pay and app payment on a bit of paper, because the Cyclos report didn't have a till reference number, making it very difficult to reconcile each till's takings.

Then there were problems for the bookkeeper, who would have to find a way of flagging suppliers as either being paid in Bristol Pounds or in sterling, and splitting out the accounts payable report accordingly; not standard functionality in any off-the-shelf product. Whilst many bookkeeping software packages create payment files that can be automatically uploaded to any mainstream bank, saving time and keying errors, the Bristol Pound payments had to be keyed in one by one. There were security issues, as there was only one login per Cyclos account, meaning that for businesses with more than one member of staff involved in doing the accounts, there was a lack of security and audit trail for transactions made on the system. There was no ability to have one person enter transactions and someone else authorise them (a way of working that is common in business to help avoid fraud). There were also cash flow issues - if a business had money tied up in a Bristol Pound account and needed to access it, it often took over a day (because of the batch update process already mentioned) to get the money transferred to the main bank account. And then there was a niggling pressure from the Bristol Pound team on businesses to change their suppliers to keep the Bristol Pounds circulating.

Let's just think about that from a business's perspective.

Say I make brownies. My unique selling point (USP) is that mine are the best brownies in the city. I've honed a recipe over several years. Thanks to trial and error, I've found the very best chocolate, cocoa, nuts, butter, eggs, sugar and flour. I've built up really good relationships with my suppliers for each of these products. If my suppliers are working well for me, why would I risk changing them? If it ain't broke, don't fix it! Let's say I do change my chocolate supplier, and therefore the brand of chocolate I'm using too. My brownies don't taste quite the same. I start to get the shops that stock my brownies contacting me, saying they're not selling as well and they've had some disappointed customers. I go back to my erstwhile supplier, but she's rather cross with me. The trust is gone. She is happy to supply me again, but the special discounted price she used to offer me has been withdrawn and she's no longer prepared to rush round with last-minute orders as a favour. Businesses are highly reliant on their suppliers. They don't mess with them lightly.

What if I've got to choose a new supplier? Maybe then I would be happy to consider a Bristol Pound business first? Probably not. What matters to me when choosing a supplier is cost, quality, accreditations, lead time, and whether I trust them—in short, everything is more important to me than the payment method.

Despite all this, many businesses still liked the idea of local businesses supporting each other and were broadly supportive of us. But unless membership brought the business some benefits, they couldn't really justify being part of it.

The research did find some clear areas of opportunity where we could bring benefits based on the difficulties small businesses were facing. These included networking and peer support, access to business advice, and help with marketing, in particular digital marketing. Amazingly, businesses even suggested they would pay for a membership that helped them meet their needs in these areas.

This gave us some ideas. We could create a new membership package for businesses that met some of their needs. The offer would include invitations to regular networking events, with presentations that small businesses would find helpful, on topics like employing people for the first time, or understanding VAT. Businesses offering services in those areas would probably be prepared to do the occasional short presentation for free, as it might land them new clients. Meanwhile, we could run promotional campaigns for members using our social media accounts, which for a small organisation had surprisingly large followings. We would let them have customisable listings on our website, interview them and write blogs, focusing on creating copy that they could use and adapt for their own digital marketing. We immediately started holding regular networking breakfasts, inviting member businesses and council officers to present on topics that would interest our members, for example, how to tender to provide services to the council. Then we started to hone our new offer for businesses, getting feedback from potential new members to get the price and the service offer just right.

It all seemed very promising, but we needed some kind of re-launch to show that we were doing something new. We needed help to develop new branding and marketing. Luckily, we soon had access to just the support we needed.

DIANA FINCH

SETsquared Incubator

The Bristol Pound office had first been set up in the Corn Exchange building, home to St Nicholas Market. Soon after I joined, we received notice to quit by May 2019. The council said the building was to be sold, and would probably be turned into a luxury hotel. The hunt for a new home began. The Engine Shed looked promising, and in particular SETsquared, which was based there. SETsquared offered office space through membership to its incubator programme. This was just what we needed; expert help to try to grow the business and cheap rent (by Bristol office standards). We applied and I had to be interviewed: did Bristol Pound really fit their remit, which was about growing tech-based startups? We'd been going ten years—hardly a startup—and our tech was decidedly out of date. But somehow, I made the case that we were doing something innovative and that we were a sort of non-profit fintech enterprise. To my amazement, they accepted us into their fold. We moved offices in April 2019 and started to make use of the many professional advisors that supported the incubator, starting with our need to present a new offer for businesses.

I met with Tanya from Estrella Green, the company providing marketing support to SETsquared members. I was full of hope. That hope disappeared within five minutes of the meeting starting. Tanya did not mince her words. She explained that the Bristol Pound brand was Marmite—you either loved it or hated it. And many people hated it. Why? Because it sounded judgemental, cliquey and arcane. If we wanted to relaunch, we needed to lose the rather academic and zealous explanations of what we were doing and focus instead on a simple message with a value proposition. And not just for businesses; for individuals too. She also described the currency itself as a hair shirt, an uncomfortable thing requiring significant pain on the part of the user. There was an undeniable hassle factor—committing to using the currency made life both more complicated and more costly—and this would always put people off. She explained that changing a brand that has been around for 10 years and that people already have strong feelings about is not easy, and that many rebrands fail. Tanya suggested we start drafting potential straplines, messages and calls to action, and run some focus groups to learn a bit more about what resonated. It was a busy summer doing all that!

In a way, Tanya's synopsis should not have been a surprise. We had done some research in 2014 that I had already come across, looking at the demographics of who was using the currency. What we had found was that 44% of individual users had a PhD, and over 82% had at least a first academic degree. 72% were in professional or managerial jobs. We were attracting people who had the luxury of making choices about how they spent their money based on something other than cost, and who were educated enough to question the functioning of our global economic system. When I approached Bristol City Council (by then Labour-controlled) for funding soon after I joined the organisation, they pointed out that the user base did not reflect the demographics of the city. I tried the argument that I didn't care how affluent the currency's individual users were as long as they were being encouraged to support our independent business members, who were primarily situated in the poorer parts of the city. Arguably, the richer the individual members were, the better!

But I could see their point. A community currency really ought to be accessible to the whole community.

It's worth noting that not all local currencies have this problem, especially in other parts of the world where the authorities take a more proactive and visionary approach. For example, with the REC in Barcelona and with most of the fairly new local currencies in South Korea, the local governments give out some social benefits in the local currency. In this way, they not only widen the usage of the currency, but more importantly, they get double the bang for their buck. First, poorer people are supported, and then local businesses are supported too. Perhaps if Bristol City Council had been more willing to think creatively about how the infrastructure could be used, the Bristol Pound story could have been very different. Imagine if instead of providing funding to food banks, the local currency was distributed to people in food poverty, and local traders encouraged to set up markets in areas of social need. Instead of creating a dependency on food banks, which undermine local food businesses and remove people's ability to choose what they eat, a totally different solution to food poverty could be created, with less damaging results. Anyway, as it was, the council did give us some short-term grant funding, but they did nothing to help the currency create the impacts they and we would have liked to see.

Tanya's summary tied in with conversations I'd had with local people. As part of our outreach work, we'd often have stalls at fairs and festivals so we'd get the chance to talk about what we were doing with a wide range of individuals. I would often get asked why someone should join. They were really asking about what was in it for them. Were there loyalty rewards, like they'd get with their Tesco Clubcard, or Nectar points? The answer was that there was nothing; the only reason that you'd join is because you thought it was important to support local businesses rather than large national and international chain stores. Local independent businesses were already struggling, and we couldn't make it even harder for them by insisting they give a discount when people paid in Bristol Pounds. Some member businesses did offer discounts and special offers to people paying in Bristol Pounds, feeling that the marketing boost would overall increase their turnover. But most did not, and would not have joined the scheme if we had put even more requirements on them. And without discounts, what we were proposing made no sense to most people, who are understandably far more concerned with the cost of living than with some minuscule impact they might potentially have on the economic system.

All that said, rethinking the branding and value proposition was clearly important for the new business services. Alongside running the focus groups, we approached Intercity Studio to think about how we could refresh the visual brand. They came up with a range of options, reimagining our old logo representing a B and a £ sign, and suggesting colour schemes and fonts. We went for something that looked business-friendly and unfussy.

At last, in September 2019, we were ready for the relaunch. We had some limited success, which spurred us on. For the first time in a couple of years, businesses were actively contacting us and wanting to join, even though we were asking them for money. And for the first time ever, it seemed we had a way of recruiting business members without losing money on every single sign up!

Growth

The scale of the success of the relaunch must not be overstated; the numbers were still small, and we needed to grow usage by a factor of fifty, you will remember, if we were to stand any chance of being viable as a currency operation. It was time to talk to James Berry at BCU about our intention to scale up operations. This was when I learned for the first time about some of the problems with our reliance on the BCU as Bristol Pound's regulated entity.

It was bad news. First, James explained that the batch update process that kept Cyclos in line with BCU's accounts was even clunkier than I'd imagined. It took a person, generally him, to sit by the computer during the update, resolving any issues on the fly, so that the programme could complete. From a time and resources perspective, the current tech could not cope with a fifty-fold increase in transactions.

Worse, if the operation were to scale up by a factor of fifty, even if the money circulated better, the level of balances held on the accounts in BCU would take them well over their own regulatory limits. Talking to James, I learned that Credit Unions have tight regulations on the ratio of reserves to deposits. Even to increase deposits of Bristol Pounds by a factor of five would mean the credit union having to raise significant investment to strengthen their balance sheet. Quite simply, if we wanted to scale up to enough to become viable, we'd have to find a new partner or become regulated in our own right.

But then James pointed out a problem with that too: the contract we had with BCU was in perpetuity and exclusive. The only way we could terminate the contract was by having a dispute. And before we started such a process, we needed to be sure we had a new solution ready to go.

Fundraising

From the moment I joined the organisation, I met frequently with Sally Britton, one of the non-executive directors, and Ben Heald to pursue fundraising opportunities. One of our best prospects, we thought, was to get more funding from P4NE. But before we could apply, I needed to write the final grant report, which had never been filed. It wasn't a particularly easy job as the money had been spent before I joined, and I had not been part of setting the objectives that the grant was based on. It was while writing this report that I discovered for the first time that a key objective for their original grant was to create an interest-free form of finance for businesses, which we had failed to do. The plan of course had been to create Prospects, but that had not come to fruition. More recently, there had been another plan that would meet the objective, but that was still in development (more on this in a moment). Let's just say that my final report to P4NE did not make for happy reading, and when I spoke to them about reapplying for funding, they explained politely that such an application would not be well received.

We continued to apply to various funders over the next few years, testing out alternative approaches, thinking of different objectives and potential impacts we felt we could measure and deliver. But no charitable trusts funded us after I joined the organisation, with the exception of Friends Provident Foundation, who gave us £5,000 (thanks to an application put in by Sally Britton just before I joined) to run a roundtable event on the future of local currencies in the autumn of 2018. I sometimes wonder if I was just rubbish at fundraising, but then I remember that during my time in the voluntary sector, I did raise hundreds of thousands of pounds in grants and secured a few million through tendering processes for service level agreements. So I don't think it was just down to me, though I can't rule this out!

Interest-free Business Loans

Let's return to the belated solution we developed to deliver on the promise of interest-free loans for businesses that was such a key outcome for the P4NE funding. The idea was that BCU could lend money to businesses at 0% interest. Meanwhile, to cover the cost of the interest it was foregoing, a transaction charge would be made on any invoices paid with the proceeds of the loan. Let's work through an example:

- I decide to refurbish my cafe. I get some quotes and I find a supplier (who is eligible to be a business member) who says he can do it for £12k.

- I say that's good, but that he'll have to pay a 5% (£600) transaction charge out of it, so he'll only get £11,400. Luckily, he says he's fine with that; it's a cost he's prepared to pay to secure the new business.

- I apply for the loan from BCU. They check my credit rating before putting the money into a special account. Meanwhile, they set up another account showing the money I owe them, which I have to pay off within a year.

VALUE BEYOND MONEY

- The work gets done and the supplier puts in his bill. I pay it from the loaned money, and BCU skim off £600 from the £12k when they process the payment.

- Meanwhile, I start paying £1k a month for a year to repay the loan.

From BCU's perspective, the 5% transaction charge needs to cover what they would have earned in interest on a normal loan. At the point all this was being worked out, the assumption was that BCU would charge 6% interest per annum. What would they normally have earned on a £12k loan being paid off at a rate of £1k per month? The answer is about £407 in compound interest. They would also normally have charged a loan arrangement fee of £75. So, as long as the loan is paid off promptly, BCU will be happy, as with this new model, they'll get £600 instead of the £482 they would have expected with a normal loan. However, if I'm late paying back my loan—and I have little incentive to pay it off quickly, in accordance with the agreement, since it is interest-free—things might look very different to BCU. If it takes me 18 months to pay it back, BCU is probably out of pocket on what it would normally earn on a loan.

Why does BCU have to earn money on the loan? Well, partly that is how they make the money to run their business. But also they have to be able to cover the costs of anyone defaulting on their loans. There is a not insignificant risk in lending money to small businesses, and BCU had not been set up to deliver commercial loans, so to them it felt even more risky, with the potential of impacting negatively on their primary community of users, namely people living with various degrees of poverty.

Despite this increased risk, BCU was prepared to go ahead with a trial of the interest-free business loans. It took Nic Hemley and Owen Davis quite some time to get the tech all working. Meanwhile, I had to get the paperwork, processes, and necessary insurance in place. It sapped James Berry's time too, ensuring every part of the approval process and Cyclos development would work from their perspective in terms of risk management and regulation. Eventually, we launched the loans in spring 2019.

A year on, and not one business had applied. We closed the loans scheme. Why did no businesses apply? There were several barriers we had not thought about too much from the businesses' perspective. The main one was that they had to have their entire supply chain for the project they were seeking funding for in place before they could apply, and that supply chain had to be exclusively businesses who were eligible and willing to become business members.

It was a neat and novel approach, where the businesses who benefited from the new businesses—the suppliers—paid for the investment, rather than the business taking a risk in trying to develop their own business.

You could say we'll never know if our novel interest-free loans could have worked, because nobody ever tried using them. But I think that it is more honest to say that they clearly didn't work because no businesses even applied.

CHAPTER SIX - WHAT NEXT?

*In which we explore some alternatives
to operating a local currency*

By late autumn of 2019, it was clear that saving the Bristol Pound was not going to be achievable. We had tried a re-launch, and had sought to re-define our offer to small businesses. Whilst this had improved membership and business usage slightly, it was insufficient to make the currency viable. Plus, we would need massive investment (at least £400k[15]) in tech and regulation to have a system that could operate at the level needed to make it viable, but nobody was prepared to give us funding for that. We knew we had to keep the paper currency in circulation until the end of September 2021, as the notes had already been printed with that expiry date. So, we had a couple of years of continued existence, and we wanted to make the best use of that time.

We had a decision to make. We could just limp on with Bristol Pound until the notes expired, then close down the CIC and give any remaining funds to the Transition Network, as set out in our governing document. Alternatively, we could use the remaining funds and time to try to do something else.

On balance, there was a feeling that the global economic and

---

15 This would be to cover software development, professional fees incurred in the regulation process, as well as staff time for two to three years, to implement and market the new offer.

environmental situation that had compelled the founders to start the Bristol Pound had only got worse in the intervening period. Inequity was still increasing and the climate crisis was being accelerated faster than ever by the growth in use of fossil fuels.

There seemed to be two possible directions for development. One was to continue to focus on localisation, but this time to try to do something that would actually be useful for local businesses. The other was to do something completely different with money.

At first, a club for small businesses seemed most viable. We already had a basic offer for businesses and could imagine ways of developing that. However, we recognised that it was a fairly crowded market. The Federation of Small Businesses and government funded initiatives like Outset had business support covered, whilst the Chamber of Commerce and groups like BNI (Business Network International) offered great networking that we couldn't match. It felt hard to carve out a niche where we could offer a unique proposition.

I started to develop some ideas around an offering for small businesses when that still seemed a likely way forward. I met Kostas Iatridis at the University of Bath. Kostas had a group of international students undertaking an MSc in Sustainability and Management and was looking for project ideas for them. I felt I had identified a gap in the market that might provide a useful project.

There was plenty of help for big businesses wanting to make their operations more sustainable, but if you were running a small business, it was difficult to know where to start. If you had money to spare, you could pay a specialist consultancy firm to work out your carbon footprint. If you didn't, your only option was to do hours of online training, first to understand all the jargon and then to work out what to do. Most small businesses have neither spare money nor spare time. The United Nations Sustainable Development Goals (SDGs) seemed to be driving much of the work that bigger businesses were doing to improve their green credentials, so I suggested that the students might like to work on an SDG aligned tool to help small businesses become greener.

The important thing was the tool should require no expertise on environmental matters on the part of the business owner, and take minutes, rather than hours, to fill in. It should not require the business owner to look up any figures, like their electricity bills for the last year, or whatever. The tool should provide the businesses with a grade (which I thought would be a sort of accreditation on the business's profile on our platform), and some pointers as to what they could do next to improve their performance.

It turned out to be a more complex task than we'd first imagined, and Kostas continued the project with his next cohort of students, taking the best ideas from the first cohort and asking the second cohort to develop them further. The resulting prototype questionnaire was really impressive. It was flexible enough to work for any business owner, whether an accountancy firm or a bakery, a shop or a garage. The questions were grouped into modules that could be skipped if they weren't relevant. For example, there was a section on employees and another on premises which would just be omitted depending on the answer to the initial basic questions. Most businesses took about 10 to 20 minutes to fill it in. The questionnaire not only looked at obvious things like energy-saving measures, but also considered business models. For example, in the section covering manufacturing, there was a question about whether the business was focused on making a quality product that would be repairable, or on making a cheaper product that might mean that people had to replace it sooner. I showed the tool to the Federation of Small Businesses, and they were quite excited about it.

Meanwhile, I had been having an exciting year learning more about how to change the financial system to improve outcomes for people and planet. It was this that helped make the decision: the next project should do something meaningful with money, rather than focusing on small businesses.

Finance Innovation Lab

In mid-October 2018, Marloes Nicholls from The Finance Innovation Lab (FIL) contacted me to ask if I'd like to speak at their Bristol event later that month. I talked to her about some of the ideas we were examining, including a potential one Nic Hemley had formulated: to create a sort of local stock exchange on a blockchain, so that people could invest in local small businesses by buying shares. Marloes suggested I might like to apply to be on their fellowship programme, and she came up with lots of other ideas that the programme might help us to explore. Had we thought about what the new open banking regulations could do to improve the Bristol Pound offer? Had we thought about the potential of using our data for good, rather than for commercial gain, to create a valuable resource for communities?

I duly went along to the event, and Marloes spoke to me

VALUE BEYOND MONEY

again, encouraging me to apply for the fellowship. I mentioned it at the next board meeting. There was no money for this kind of personal development, and even if I were successful in getting a free place (there were some available) it would impact on my work time significantly because I wasn't full time, plus the train fares would be astronomical. It seemed impossible. But then Marloes said there were some bursaries that could help cover the travel, and I realised that the fact that I wasn't full time, and didn't have many other commitments, meant that I could attend in my own time. The board agreed that I could apply on those terms. So it was that, a few weeks later, I found myself at their boot camp in London, which was part of their selection process. There were about thirty of us. The event started with a brief meditation. I'd never been to anything quite like it before. Then there were team building exercises and the opportunity to pitch our ideas to each other. I had imposter syndrome, as the ideas I was pitching were ones I'd inherited and were not really my own. I felt very lucky to be selected.

The Fellowship alone deserves a whole book. It was a fantastic opportunity to learn about the financial system through the eyes of both Finance Innovation Lab staff and a variety of invited speakers who were all in their own way challenging the existing financial system. The other Fellows[16] were really inspirational too, bravely pursuing ideas for services that could either disrupt the current financial system or at least make it work better for those who are usually either ignored or damaged by it. One of my favourites was the Equal Care Co-op, who are working to revolutionise the domiciliary

---

16   https://financeinnovationlab.org/our-work/fellowship/alumni/

care sector by empowering both care givers and care receivers using a platform co-op approach. This is a direct challenge to the usual corporate approach through which both staff and clients are disrespected and undervalued. Over the course of the following nine months, we became a close group, particularly on the intensive retreats. The Fellowship was as much about growing us as resilient, heart-driven individuals as about helping us develop our respective projects and spot the points of leverage in a ubiquitous system that defines and controls economic power.

New ways of thinking about money and value

It was during the course of the Fellowship that I met someone who really opened my eyes to the potential future direction for local currencies. Farid Tejani was at one of the first events I attended, and he quickly offered to come to Bristol to talk through the exciting ideas he had about using blockchain technology in combination with local currencies. A few weeks later, he met with Nic and myself and blew our minds. We went down to a café in St Nick's market, and Farid started to explain that he felt there was scope to use tokens on a blockchain to enable very different sorts of relationships between customers and traders. I have to say, I understood very little of what Farid said the first few times I spoke with him. Just the terms "blockchain" and "token" were enough to make me come out in a cold sweat. Luckily, Nic was able to demystify things between the meetings, and gradually I started to see the potential of the sorts of ideas that Farid was developing.

The purpose of this book is not to explain how a blockchain

works from a technical perspective. Rather, what is pertinent to this book is what a blockchain can be used for and what its functionality is as a tool. A blockchain provides a special sort of database where there is no reliance on one trusted party (such as a bank or software company) to control or maintain the data. Rather, all parties with access can record data to the blockchain directly. Meanwhile, the way the data is held, distributed across many different servers, makes it almost impossible to hack or falsify. It's sometimes called "trustless", because there is no trust invested in one company or authority to maintain the data. The data itself is meanwhile more trustworthy, because nobody has the power to tamper with previously recorded data.

When I mention blockchains, most people immediately assume I'm talking about crypto-currencies. I am not. This is not the place for a debate on crypto-currencies. But to clarify, perhaps it is useful to summarise that crypto-currencies are a form of privately created money held on a trustless distributed database. Bank money is also privately created, but many people don't trust banks, and think that money held on a blockchain is therefore preferable. This is understandable, as banks have all the power over their ledgers but ultimately have their own interests at heart. On the plus side though, at least banks have to abide by regulations. There are rules about the level of reserves they must have. There are processes they must abide by to help prevent money laundering and to ensure they know who account holders really are. The purpose of the regulations is to protect people who are storing their money in the bank, particularly from the potential of the bank failing and losing all their money.

Crypto-currencies might not rely on us trusting a bank with our financial affairs, but they are inherently more risky because there is precious little regulation covering them, and generally no "real" money (dollars in a vault referenced on a balance sheet, say) backing up the money on the system. If the crypto-currency ceases operating, or becomes valueless, everybody loses all the money they've invested.

If I'm not talking about crypto-currencies, what am I talking about? I'm talking about using tokens on a blockchain to create a trustless record of things other than money. More on this later, but for now let's just say that these conversations with Farid made me feel that, rather than focusing on creating services for small businesses after the Bristol Pound operation had finished, we should be thinking about potential uses for blockchain tokens that could help Bristol's economy become better in terms of its environmental and social performance. This would be in keeping with the underlying drivers behind creating local currencies like the Bristol Pound, but would free us from focusing on localisation as our only approach. It would also be radical and potentially game-changing, as Prospects had hoped to be, and thus in keeping with the spirit of the original project.

Learnings From The Bristol Pound

Before we could start designing what would come next, we needed to reflect on what the key problems were with the Bristol Pound. Whatever we did next might well fail, but it would be a real waste of time if it failed for the same reasons as the Bristol Pound. What were the pitfalls to avoid?

The first thing was that we must ensure that we could attract enough users of the new product to give it a chance of success. With Bristol Pound, we had managed to attract about 0.2% of Bristol's population to think of setting up an account. Of those, about 10% actually used it; 0.02% of the population. As already mentioned, Bristol Pound was a Marmite brand, which explains the very low take up. But how had we managed to come up with such a brand position?

The early Bristol Pound team, seeking to build adoption of their new product, did what any startup company would do: they tried to appeal to the "low-hanging fruit" who would be the early adopters. In most startup companies, where the main driver for adoption of their product is the promise of meeting an unmet need, this is a good strategy. The early adopters are keen to experiment and likely to be forgiving of any teething problems. Gradually, the product is improved in line with feedback from the early adopters, and is perhaps shaped to meet other unmet needs that have been identified by them in the interim, making it more appealing to a wider range of customers. But the Bristol Pound was not a typical startup. The product it created was not meeting a particular need of its users. The only reason you would use the Bristol Pound was if a certain "new economy" ideology resonated with you. The early adopters would not be people who needed a solution to a common problem they all faced; they would be people who had similar views to the founders about the problem with our economic system. They would be people who felt strongly enough about the need to localise trade that they were prepared to wear the hair shirt, to put themselves out and use the new currency.

I think the problem that Bristol Pound created for itself is actually a common one for social movements. A group of people who care passionately about something and want to create a movement start by explaining what their thinking is. They try to appeal to other people who think like them, to get them to come on board. The plan they have is that momentum will just keep growing the movement from there. Gradually, more and more people will see the light, they believe, not least because everyone they talk to in the growing group agrees that what they're proposing is obvious.

But there is a problem with this assumption. As soon as you define what it is you care about, and get the people who think like you signing up, you have created a boundary. People who don't think like you will find it hard to cross over. Indeed, the more you shout about what you believe in, the more you alienate yourselves from the mainstream, and the less likely you are to get people who don't think like you to join you. This is perhaps seen particularly well with XR (Extinction Rebellion), whose initial direct actions became so big and caused such a nuisance to so many people with mainstream views that they alienated many, including some of the people who agreed with their environmental and social justice aims.

The key learning for us was that, whatever project followed the Bristol Pound, it must not rely on ideology to create its usership. It must have a low bar to entry, rather than create a barrier by effectively saying, "If you're as woke as us, you can join!" Whatever the marketing call to action was, it would need to work with a mainstream audience who understand things within the current paradigm. It must also have a USP that would appeal to lots of people, not just a small minority, and offer a value proposition that would resonate with many people. We had to find a solution to something that lots of people would agree was a problem.

This was a conundrum. Clearly the Bristol Pound's aims are highly ideological. We want to change the world by getting people and businesses to think and behave differently. We want to take people on a journey of change. Surely, it is inconceivable that with those aims, we would choose not to start with a call to action based on our beliefs?

Let's consider the success or otherwise of Bristol Pound in changing behaviours. Did we take people on a journey? Did they change their behaviour because of the Bristol Pound? I expect we did give an extra prod to our members to shop at locally-owned businesses, but the reality is that most people who joined the Bristol Pound already thought that shopping at local businesses was important. Indeed, when we asked businesses whether they'd got many new customers thanks to signing up to the Bristol Pound, most told us they hadn't. Rather, they told us that some of their existing customers had simply changed to paying with Bristol Pounds. So perhaps recruiting people who already thought like us meant that we didn't actually change their behaviour very much. And we certainly weren't changing the behaviour of people who didn't think like us. If we found a way to recruit users to the new product who didn't already think like us, we'd actually be more likely to take them on a journey of change.

A slight caveat to the last thought. We did run an impact survey of our currency users in 2019. We asked what other changes people and businesses had made in their lives after starting using the currency. The response rates weren't great, so the findings may not be representative, but still the results were interesting. Many of the changes individual users reported were expected, such as the high proportion of them that had changed where they shopped and switched to one of the energy suppliers on the scheme. But many were buying more second-hand goods, had begun growing their own vegetables or keeping chickens, and had changed their bank account. Some had even moved their pension investments. These things weren't changes that were directly attributable to the functioning of the currency, but they suggested that we had encouraged users of the currency to think differently about their impact as actors within the current economic system. Similarly, most businesses had changed their purchasing policies, as we might have expected. But significant numbers had also changed their human resource policies and, like the individual members, moved their bank accounts, suggesting some unexpected outcomes of the Bristol Pound.

At a wider level, let's consider whether Bristol Pound achieved any of its original aims. Had it helped to create a vibrant, diverse and resilient local economy? Had it localised the economy in any measurable way? Had it reduced transport-related carbon emissions? The short answer is no. At least, not as far as anyone can tell. Partly this might be a data problem; there was nothing you could measure to evidence any impact. But even if there were city-wide data we could look at, it is highly unlikely that we would be able to spot a "Bristol Pound effect". Indeed, how could there be any measurable effect with 0.02% of the population of Bristol occasionally shopping at local shops, especially when they were probably doing that already?

VALUE BEYOND MONEY

Don't get me wrong, the Bristol Pound had an impressive track record as a local currency and made lots of other impacts that weren't foreseen. It helped the city become the European Green Capital in 2015. It became renowned worldwide as the first local currency to operate at a city scale, was the first to enable payment of local taxes (both business rates and council tax) in a local currency, and the first to have digital and paper money from the outset. Many people around the world were inspired by Bristol Pound's apparent success story. Academics as far afield as Japan and Chile studied it. Many staff and founders whom I interviewed emphasised how successful it had been and how proud they were to have been part of such an influential and famous project. But in terms of doing the things it had set out to do, there was no substantive proof that it had achieved anything.

I'd like to put in a little caveat here too, as that last sentence would be enough to put anyone off trying to start a local currency scheme. Whilst we did not have access to transaction data because of BCU's data protection rules, in the summer of 2019 we did get permission for an independent researcher, Mark Thurstain-Goodwin, to look at the business-to-business digital transaction data. With some very fancy visualisation tools, Mark was able to demonstrate the emergence of loops as the network of businesses grew and diversified. By 2016, every business in the network was linked to every other business through a chain of transactions. Mark's diagrams also clearly show that as businesses left the network, which started happening in 2017, the relationships between businesses started to break down, and the network became increasingly fragmented again.

DIANA FINCH

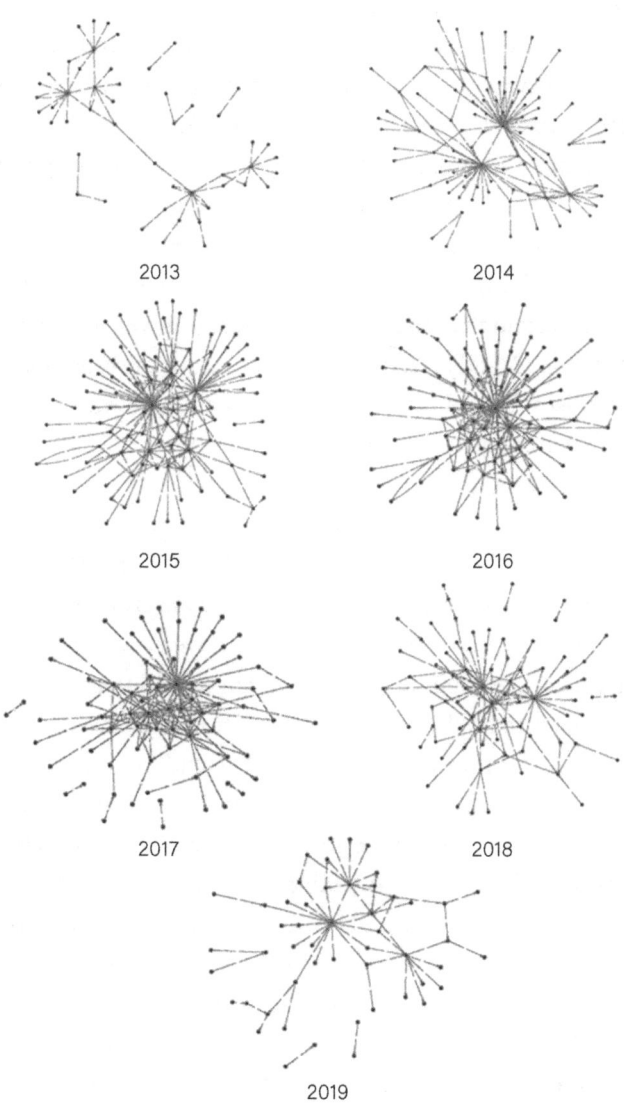

Diagrams showing the development of the
Bristol Pound B2B network, M Thurstain-Goodwin

VALUE BEYOND MONEY

There were some businesses that were particularly well connected—key nodes if you like—and these tended to be either wholesalers or businesses offering services that are needed across many sectors, like accountants. Within this, Mark found particular evidence of localisation emerging in the food sector supply chain. Of course, it is possible that many of these connections already existed, and were just made visible by the Bristol Pound transaction data. Equally, it is almost certain that many of the connections were enabled by the network. Exactly how much impact can be fairly attributed to the Bristol Pound is a question we cannot answer. I would say, however, that being able to see and measure localisation is an important metric in its own right if we are going to localise our economies. A currency is not the only way of achieving this, though. Michael Hallam's work on "The Local Loop" in Lancaster was able to measure localisation by getting participating businesses to share their sales and purchase invoice data. Through the analysis of that data, he was also able to demonstrate the local multiplier effect in operation.

For whatever project we did next, it would be important to think about our impact from the outset. We'd need lots of people to join, we'd need them all to make some small change to their behaviour, and we'd need to be able to capture data to show the impact that was being created. Creating impact would help us to raise funds, and would potentially drive adoption too.

We also needed the next project to be easy and engaging. Rather than be a hair shirt—asking people to do something that would add pain to their daily lives—we needed to be a cosy jumper, encouraging people to do something that would be enjoyable and useful.

Finally, we would need to make sure we had access to our own data so that we could see what was working and what wasn't. I'm sure most startups take this for granted, but after the experience of not having access to our data on the Bristol Pound, this was definitely something on our minds.

CHAPTER SEVEN
A NEW PROJECT

In which we decide on a way forward

When we first started to think about how we could create a project that had mainstream appeal and got people to change an aspect of their behaviour, we were stumped. As soon as we explained what we wanted people to do, it would become ideological and limit our ability to engage with a wide audience.

Then came the brainwave: we could develop something that had a really simple call to action and not tell them what the real aim of the product was. We could sneak in our real purpose as an add-on that people might just try out for fun. The project must therefore have two parts. First, there would be the part with a strong and simple marketing message and a business and operational model that would work at scale. Second, there would be the part that actually made an impact on the things we cared about.

Many people couldn't grasp this concept. Over the next three years, talking over our ideas with a range of business advisors, as well as potential partners and funders, people kept saying that we were developing two projects and that we should separate them. From their standard business perspective, there was one strong attractive and scalable business proposition, and one niche project for "green" people with no discernible business plan. Most of them thought we should just drop the niche green project and go with the strong business proposition. But from our perspective, that would be selling out. We weren't interested in creating a payment business just for the sake of it. The whole point was to create impact.

Bristol Pay

So, what was the scalable strong business proposition that would be easy to market and make money? The answer was a payment platform based on Electronic Money Institution regulations. It was this functionality that drove the choice of name, first mooted as Local Pay, and eventually known as Bristol Pay. We also used the name City Pay, particularly when we were explaining how the City Pay infrastructure could be used to support local implementations all over the country and beyond, with the local implementations taking the name of the place where they operated (Exeter Pay, Manchester Pay, Bordeaux Pay, and so on). From here on, I'm going to refer to the new project as Bristol Pay.

When I pay with a card or phone at a shop, the shop has to pay a fee on the transaction. The level of the fee varies depending on the provider of the payment service. Some providers make the shop owner buy a fairly cheap card reader and then pay a higher percentage on each transaction. Others demand a high service charge to hire the card reader, which might be integrated into a fancy terminal that assists with other business functions, and then charge a lower percentage on each transaction. But for ease, let's say that, whatever the deal, it's generally going to equate to a cost of between 1% and 3% on every transaction.

The reason for this fee is that for the money to get from, say, my bank account, which happens to be at Triodos, to the bank account of the shop I'm at, which for argument's sake might be with the Cooperative Bank, a whole load of third parties have to get involved, and they all need paying for the services they are providing.

First, there's the card issuer, with VISA and Mastercard being the main players. They provide me with a card, which costs money to produce and keep secure. They also provide the bank with some tech so that payments on that card hit my bank account fairly seamlessly. The tech ensures that the card issuer receives payment for all the charges made on that bank's customers' cards that day.

Second, there is the provider of the point of sale payment service, who have to develop both hardware and software to ensure that my card details can be read, approval from the card provider sought (linking all the way back to the bank's ledgers to ensure there are sufficient funds or a high enough credit limit for the transaction), and payment taken, with the net proceeds (that is, the sale value minus the transaction charge) being transferred to the shop's bank account (usually batched up and paid once a day).

Then there are all the intervening payment clearing services, because in reality each card issuer batches up payments relating to each payment service provider on a periodic basis. Data about each transaction, date and time of payment, customer and merchant) is then needed for all the reconciliations of these batched payments. Just to complicate matters, sometimes more than one payment provider is used. For example, these days when we pay by PayPal, we can choose whether the money should come from a particular card, from our PayPal balance, or from our bank account.

This payment infrastructure is an open system; any customer's bank account can be used to transfer funds to any merchant's bank account, without having to exchange bank details. Even though the funds aren't transferred instantly at the point of sale, there is sufficient trust in the system that merchants can act as if they've received payment instantly. It's therefore highly convenient for customers and merchants. However, it's also quite costly to run, as this simplified explanation of what is actually happening under the bonnet suggests. Worse, it's very open to fraud because there are so many moving parts, and because no merchant has a direct link with any customer.

EMI providers take a different approach. They have both customers and merchants on their own platform, creating a closed payment system. This is like the original PayPal model, although PayPal predated the EMI regulation in the UK. I can transfer money into my PayPal account from my bank. I can then transfer that money to another PayPal user without any other banks or payment providers being involved. The recipient of my money can then download it to their bank account. PayPal can verify the identity of both payer and recipient, making it easier to avoid fraudulent activity. And for PayPal, moving the money between accounts is very cheap—it's just a journal entry between two accounts on their ledger. PayPal is successful despite charging a lot for its services, because it's become so handy for online payments. Instead of needing to remember my card or bank details, which are long and complicated, I just need to remember my email address and password to make a payment online by PayPal. And PayPal has also automated the link to its customers' bank accounts, so that I can make a payment even if I haven't got money on my PayPal account, as the funds will be automatically taken from my bank thanks to the direct debit mandate I've signed with PayPal.

PayPal is a commercial organisation and prices its services based on what the market will stand. It is therefore a highly profitable company. The business model for EMI operations is undoubtedly strong.

So, this was our idea: we would operate a closed loop payment platform a bit like PayPal. Payments we processed would have a low cost per transaction as we would just be doing a journal entry between two accounts on our own system. We could charge merchants at a competitive rate, and should therefore be able to make a surplus on the operation. The USP would be that instead of being just another commercial operator like PayPal, we would be a non-profit payment platform. Unlike any other payment provider, we would give away any surpluses we made to local charities and voluntary sector service providers.

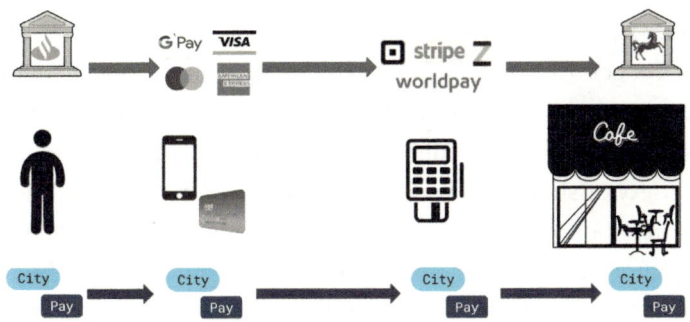

Open loop vs closed loop payment system

The question was, how much money could we potentially raise for the voluntary sector? Would it be enough to make our USP sound compelling?

In early 2020, we were introduced to Payji Ltd. They were a new startup focused on creating payment technology to improve the deal for small businesses and were keen to develop an EMI regulated payment service for us. They did quite a bit of data modelling to work out how much money is being lost to Bristol each year in electronic consumer payments. The answer was pretty staggering: somewhere between £45 million and £90 million every year, depending on the data set and assumptions used. Of course, since COVID-19 there has been a further shift towards electronic payment methods, so this figure is likely to have gone up.

We calculated that if we managed to get 5% market penetration in the city, this might mean we could bring in around £3 million every year. Assuming a cost of £500,000 to run the operation, that would leave £2.5 million for local voluntary sector services. A 10% penetration would mean over £5 million in funds raised.

To get that kind of market penetration, we needed to be sure that our USP really resonated with people. In the summer of 2020, we did some market research. We asked a variety of shops and hospitality businesses in the city if they would be prepared to offer consumers a second payment method (with similar costs to their current payment method) if that additional payment method raised money for the local voluntary sector. All the businesses we spoke to said yes. They said that they could see the marketing potential of being able to show their support for their local community and felt being part of such a scheme would be worth the additional complexity at the till.

For balance, we also asked whether they would be prepared to offer a second payment method if it had significantly lower transaction charges than their main payment method. The resounding response was that it would not be worth the hassle, as it would be unlikely to create any additional benefit. Most were reasonably happy with their existing payment method, and felt they had costed in the payment charges to their operations.

Payji also asked one of the major supermarket chains if they would be prepared to offer a second payment method in particular store locations that would raise funds for the voluntary sector in that location. Their response was very positive. Indeed, they said they would like a six-month exclusive period so that they would be the only national supermarket chain that could offer the payment method during that time. They felt that being able to evidence their concern for the localities where they operate was important and would help them appeal to local consumers.

As part of the market research, we also asked a variety of individuals if they would be willing to use a secondary payment method in shops and hospitality outlets that took it if that payment method would raise money (at no cost to them) for local voluntary sector organisations. They nearly all said they would be prepared to do that. Many of them were aware of the increasing reliance on the voluntary sector as cash-strapped local authorities cut back on non-statutory social services. They were therefore in favour of helping to raise money to support those voluntary sector services.

This feedback filled us with confidence that we had a winning value proposition that played well with both businesses and consumers.

There was another potential social benefit to setting up an EMI payment system for Bristol. About 2% of the adult population doesn't have a bank account, and if you don't have a bank account, you don't have access to digital money. The people affected are often poorer people, people who have been made bankrupt, or those who just don't have the types of paperwork that banks often demand to see, like utility bills in your name (which you won't have if you're living in temporary accommodation or are homeless), or a passport or a driving licence (which you won't have if you're not rich enough to travel abroad or learn to drive). This creates something of a "poverty premium". In other words, you face higher costs just because you don't have a bank account. For example, you can't shop around online to save money if you don't have digital money. You can't pay your bills by direct debit, which is the cheapest way to pay for utilities, without being connected to the banking system. There is also the problem of earning money. Most employers pay salaries directly into bank accounts. If you don't have a bank account, either you are limited to being paid in cash (which makes it more likely that you will be drawn into "cash in hand" work that does not protect your employment rights or build your National Insurance pot), or you will be reliant on someone else to receive your salary on your behalf, putting you at significant risk of financial abuse.

EMI regulation is significantly less onerous in terms of the administration and governance that is needed to set up a customer account. Indeed, at the point when we were looking into it, absolutely no "know your customer" (KYC) checks were needed if less than £125 was passing through your account in a month. You could show your ownership of the account using passwords or biometrics (like facial recognition), without any need for a verified address or identity check. Beyond that threshold, there is the potential to create proportionate checks on identity depending on the amounts of money being transacted or held. For example, if you were registered with a doctor or a charity offering support to homeless people, that might be sufficient proof to enable a slightly higher level of transactions, say £500 per month. If you were on the electoral roll, that might give you access to the top level of transactions or holdings in your account, which might be, say, £5,000 per month. The EMI can thus act as a half-way house for people not served by banks, providing digital accounts that are linked to the normal banking system through the EMI, in a similar way to building society accounts. Your bank details for receiving salaries or paying through direct debit are the bank details of the EMI with a reference number to pinpoint your account.

Thinking about specific groups that might benefit from accessing digital money, I talked to some of the charities working with asylum seekers and refugees in Bristol. They welcomed the potential of making emergency payments electronically instead of in cash. They told me about the problems the recipients of cash handouts had, often being robbed when living on the street or when staying in hostels, for example.

Points and Tokens

What about the other part of the platform; the part that would create the impact? I'll be going into a lot more detail on this soon, but just to explain it briefly, we had the idea that once you had a payment account on the platform, you could also earn various sorts of points.

Instead of being like Nectar points that you earn through shopping and that give you discounts on further shopping, these points would be earned through certain behaviours, like cycling instead of driving, and could be spent to encourage other behaviours, like going to the sports centre to improve your fitness.

Initially, we were focused on what Bristol City Council (or other local authorities) would be interested in, as we saw them as being major partners in promoting Bristol Pay. It seemed pretty obvious that they'd like the EMI payment proposal, as they had a vested interest in ensuring the voluntary sector was well funded to deliver the services it was

VALUE BEYOND MONEY

increasingly reliant on them to deliver. Beyond that, we also felt the council would need an engagement tool if they were going to be successful in delivering on various targets, such as reducing carbon emissions. The council had the ability to build infrastructures—like heat networks, recycling facilities and cycle lanes—and they could change their own buildings and policies to reduce their own carbon footprint, but that would not be enough to deliver on their city-wide targets. These would require individuals, households and businesses across the city to change their behaviour too. People have to use cycle lanes for them to be effective!

We spent a fair bit of time going through Bristol's One City Plan, which sets out a range of social and environmental targets across six themes. We were delighted to see that progress towards many targets could be helped if people and businesses were motivated to change aspects of their behaviour. Moreover, we could think of ways of earning points or tokens for many of those behaviours to create incentives. This seemed to be a strong starting point to get buy-in from the council.

The role of tokens in recognising positive actions

We then started to think about other anchor institutions across the city. NHS trusts, universities and even large corporations all had an interest in changing peoples' behaviours if they were to achieve their own environmental and/or social targets.

We even considered the needs of the very same voluntary sector services that we would be helping to fund if Bristol Pay were successful. They too had a need to engage their users in positive change. Depending on the charity, this might be anything from giving up using chemicals in the garden to control pests and weeds (and thus improve biodiversity), to engaging in more exercise (to improve health outcomes), to participating more in social activities (to improve mental health outcomes). We started to see the potential of having different types of points to count different sorts of activity for different stakeholders.

As time went on, our thinking about exactly how the points worked began to shift. But the essence of rewarding positive behaviours with some kind of point or token has remained. What got dropped from this original way of thinking was that the points needed to accrue any kind of incentive or reward, or to be spendable in some way, for reasons that will soon become clear.

The New Project Idea

The FIL Fellowship came to an end in September 2019. It was at the final event, at which each Fellow pitched their project to a roomful of potential investors, that I first presented the ideas that went on to become the focus of my work for the next three years. My pitch was mainly focused on the Bristol

Pound, but I included one slide towards the end explaining where I thought the future of Bristol Pound lay.

Just a few months later in January 2020, we pitched the more developed idea to Bristol City Council. They seemed excited. Mayor Marvin Rees said that he'd never really "got" the Bristol Pound, but he could see the potential of Bristol Pay. In particular, he felt it could engage people in parts of the city that were struggling with poverty and deprivation in a way that Bristol Pound never could.

By the end of March, we had signed an agreement with Payji Ltd to develop the EMI regulated payment technology. By coincidence, at around this time BCU told us that they would be completely replacing their account management system. This would mean either us paying lots of money to rewrite the back-end of the digital Bristol Pound system (which was not only beyond us but also pointless at this stage in our thinking), or closing the digital currency down prematurely (that is, before the paper currency expired in September 2021). It looked as though the timing might work really well with our new project. At most there might be a few months' gap between the end of the digital Bristol Pound and the start of the new Bristol Pay. Thus, the digital Bristol Pound scheme finally ended in August 2020.

Things progressed well with Payji, and in autumn 2020, we had a functioning payment platform. We recruited some local people to help us test it out. The tokens would be added later after we had got the payment platform up and running with a strong usership.

Sadly, over the winter, Payji had their own issues to contend with, which slowed down development and meant they could no longer fund us to develop the marketing, as had been the original plan. Reluctantly, we had to end the partnership with Payji in spring 2021 while we still had enough funding to try again with other potential partners and funders.

At that point, we started to think about how we could flip the phasing of the project, developing the token side of things first and adding the payments (which are the costly bit to deliver because of all the regulation) later.

Meanwhile, we had to cut our expenditure to make the money last for as long as possible. This meant losing our office space at Engine Shed, which we'd hardly used since the COVID-19 lockdown anyway, and saying goodbye to Ian Madle, who had been doing all the customer-facing work for three years. From here until the end, the team was: me, generally on 25 hours per week; Hector Steenbergen, doing communications on 2 hours a week; and the non-executive board members, who continued to donate their time to support us. It was a difficult downsizing operation from a logistical as well as an emotional perspective. Every spare bit of space in my flat was full of Bristol Pound stuff, kept just on the off chance that we'd need it again. I had a safe and laser printer in my bedroom, as well as a stack of files the size of a chest of drawers. Meanwhile, my airing cupboard was full of IT, including various routers and switches, as well as seven monitors, keyboards, and (electronic!) mice. The attic contained all the merchandise, banner stands and old accounting records. These were daily reminders of all that had once been.

In September 2021, the final series of paper Bristol Pound notes expired—nine years of beautiful notes circulating in the city ended. But we were still focused on the potential of finding some funding to pursue our new ideas, and our downsizing efforts had bought us a couple of years to find it.

CHAPTER EIGHT
TOKENOMICS

*In which we think about an economy
based on something other than money*

In the summer of 2021, we revisited the token ideas. If we were going to lead with tokens and add the payments system later, we needed to do the hard work on token design that we'd put off thus far. We started from first principles.

We found a new team to work with. Nathan Baranowski from Digital Wonderlab was keen to help us develop a prototype for the token side of the Bristol Pay app. Artist Toby Harris was excited by the idea of making dynamic graphics using token data, such that the images you'd see as part of your profile would depend on the tokens you had. We also started talking to Daniel Ames at Crown DAO, who were keen to explore use cases for their blockchain. We had a workshop in August 2021 bringing all these parties together, and started to design in earnest.

What is a Token?

In the English language, the word "token" predates the word "blockchain" by many hundreds of years. It comes from a

Germanic root meaning to "signify, show, or teach". If I give you some flowers as a "token" of my appreciation, what we mean is that the flowers represent, evidence, or signify my thanks.

Let me make it clear that the value of such a token has nothing to do with how much financial value is associated with it. The flowers I give you might have cost £50 from a florist, or they might have cost nothing. I might have snipped a couple of roses from a bush in my garden, were I to have one, or picked some wildflowers from a hedgerow when I was thinking about you. Indeed, quite possibly you'll be more touched by the free flowers that cost me nothing financially, but that showed you I had put something of myself into the choice of what to give you.

If we wanted to understand something about how much people appreciate other people in their lives and to put some kind of number on that as a measure of social cohesion, we could gather financial data on sales of flowers, boxes of chocolates, and toiletries in gift packaging. But that would only tell us the cost of gifts bought in the market economy. It would leave out the arguably more heartfelt gestures that required nothing except time, effort and thoughtfulness. Could we develop tokens to represent and count the actual social value of gratitude, which is what we were really interested in, rather than just financial values?

Are Tokens Money?

Anything can stand as a token. At various points in human history, value has been marked by artisanal and ceremonial items—including shells, animal hides and precious metals—

as well as tally sticks, coins and notes of debt. Whether all these count as money is questionable.

Money itself is a specific sort of token. It signifies a value of some sort, namely a financial value. Its movement recognises a transfer of financial value from one person to another. Money is often said to have three main functions. First, it provides a standard unit of financial value. Thanks to money, I can compare the value of apples, tables and houses in some kind of meaningful way. I could say that one apple costs 50 pence (£ 0.50), one table costs £200, and one house costs £300,000. I can say that the real living wage in the UK is so many pounds per hour. Without a standard unit of value, it would be difficult to price things consistently or pay people for their time. Second, money generally retains its value. You can store it without it deteriorating much (apart from in times of hyperinflation). Not many physical things store as well as money or retain their value as consistently. If I tried to store my wealth as wheat grain, it would go mouldy or get eaten by mice and be worthless after a few months or years. Precious metals store well, and these have therefore often been used as stores of value. However, lumps of precious metals are not as good at fulfilling the third function of money, which is that money is easy to exchange. Notes and coins, by contrast, are highly portable and easy to count. Digital money is even easier to carry and exchange, providing you have the right technology, like payment cards and smartphones.

Money is a token that meets the need of a particular purpose: trade. It is a tool for mediating the transactions of buying and selling, and for recording debts. The human race managed for many thousands of years without money; indeed, in the grand history of humanity, it is a recent invention. There are various theories as to how and why the use of money developed. We're sometimes told that it was developed to meet the increasingly complex needs of traders who started to travel between communities and deal in different commodities. Others present compelling evidence that money was developed primarily as a subjugation tool for leaders, to enable them to control and tax their subjects, thus increasing their own wealth, and in turn enabling them to accrue and exert yet more power, for example through military means.

In both of these origin stories, there is a concept of "added value" that justifies the flow of money from subjects to kings, and from customers to traders. Kings will supposedly protect their subjects by safeguarding the land on which they depend for their survival. Traders will provide for the needs of their customers. Both kings and traders are providing a service that they feel they deserve to be paid for. This is the added value. If a trader buys an item at one price, they will sell it on with a markup, as they've provided the services of procurement and delivery. Kings spend some of the money from their subjects to fund the armies that are supposedly protecting their subjects, but they keep a good chunk of it for themselves.

And so it is that over time, wealth flows to the biggest traders and the most powerful leaders. The less privileged people lose access to the land and the means of production, instead becoming reliant on waged labour to earn the money to operate within the system of taxes and purchasing. This is where we find ourselves today, with a globalised market economy and ever-growing inequality in financial wealth. In 2017, Oxfam reported that eight individuals own the same wealth as the poorest half of humanity. Meanwhile, to meet their basic needs, most people are forced to work for companies, with their productive labour helping those companies to grow, in turn increasing the flow of money from poor to rich whilst using the Earth's resources in ways that are simply not sustainable.

This market economy, driven and enabled by money, is not doing a good job of counting real value. Financial value is not real value. Alanis Obomsawin put it very nicely in the early 1970s: "When the last tree is cut, the last fish is caught, and the last river is polluted; when to breathe the air is sickening, you will realise, too late, that wealth is not in bank accounts and that you can't eat money."[17]

In short, we are busy destroying the resources of planet Earth thanks to the globalised market economy that is constantly focused on growth and the accretion of power. Once we've reduced those resources such that they no longer meet humanity's needs, no amount of money will "magic up" more resources. Rather, people, and many other creatures, will suffer and die. We are facing a mass extinction event that is likely to include ourselves. This is an existential crisis, which was seen coming in the 1970s, and which we've done nothing to avert.

Many people have had clever ideas to try to change how the market economy works. They've sought to somehow cost in the externalities that are overlooked by the current financial system: the carbon that is being emitted into our atmosphere, or the health of humans in parts of the world affected by

---

[17] As quoted in "Conversations with North American Indians" by Ted Poole in "Who is the Chairman of This Meeting?: A Collection of Essays (1972)". Source: https://quotepark.com/authors/alanis-obomsawin/

climate change and conflicts (conflicts which, all too often, have their origins in the market for resources like oil). The one that has really taken off is carbon trading. We've had carbon trading for 25 years now. Has it worked? No. Carbon dioxide emissions continue to increase, more than offsetting the growth in renewable energy sources.

Why hasn't carbon trading worked? The answer is pretty simple: we have a market economy. If companies face increased costs, either because they've had to invest to decrease their carbon usage, or because they've had to buy carbon credits, those costs get passed onto the consumer. Profit is the company's north star, and profit is still being made either way. Profit means a company can grow their operations and make more widgets. Even if they have cut their carbon footprint per widget, they are still growing their overall resource footprint because their production of widgets is increasing.

I see a difference between the real value of resources and financial values. Clean water and breathable air are things of real value. Human health and social cohesion are things of real value. Money does not count these things. Maintaining a climate and soils such that we can grow food for future generations, that is a valuable activity. And yet our market system values agricultural intensification and increased production, in turn depleting our soils, polluting our water, and causing huge emissions of CO_2 thanks to all the chemical inputs required by this model of agriculture. Building world peace is a valuable activity. But it is war that fuels the growth of the market economy through the production of weapons and the like.

If money doesn't count things of real value, could we design some tokens that would? There is a real need to start experimenting with these kinds of ideas. We won't fix the problems we've created through the market economy with yet more market economic approaches. We need a new understanding of value and new sorts of tokens of value if we are to create a different sort of economic system. Only with a completely different economic approach can we hope to fix the problems created by the market economy.

The Earth as a Commons

It is perhaps useful to bring in the idea of a commons in this context. In the past, many areas of land, like pastures for grazing animals, were managed as commons. That meant no one person owned the land. Rather, any member of the community could use the land to graze their animals. In recent times, it has been argued that commons cannot work in the long term. The "tragedy of the commons", a meme first coined by ecologist Garrett Hardin in 1968, is that some people will exploit their access to the commons for their personal gain, in turn depleting it for others and making it non-viable in the future.

As an aside, I would say that this idea of personal gain from the commons is directly linked to the operation of a market alongside the commons. If I know there is a market for my excess animals, I will indeed be tempted to grow my herd and overgraze the land this year, because that way I'll earn enough money to feed my family next year without having to spend time rearing my own animals. But if there were no such market in operation alongside the commons, what would be the point in expanding my herd and overgrazing? I would just be making it less likely that I could feed my family next year, because I'd know my animals might starve.

Elinor Ostrom worked out a set of principles that would enable any commons to be sustainable and have longevity. To summarise a few of them here:

- It must be possible to define boundaries, not only of the common resource, but in terms of who has access to it.
- The users must all be able to use their voice to exercise effective choice and control in the development of the rules for how the commons is used.
- It must be possible to monitor use of the commons so that incorrect use can be called out.
- There must be sanctions for misuse, graduated according to the severity of the misuse.
- External higher authorities must respect the commons and its rules.

Let's think of planet Earth as a commons. There is one Earth. Its resources are needed and used by all of humanity as well as other life forms. There is a clear geographical and usership boundary, albeit pretty inclusive. We need it to continue functioning in the long term, so it needs to be governed as a commons.

What is Economy?

I've got this far in the book and not given my definition of the word "economy". I know for many people that the economy is synonymous with a market economy facilitated by money.

VALUE BEYOND MONEY

For me, it isn't. I see the economy as the system by which we use the world's resources to meet the needs of its human inhabitants. It just happens that we have most recently chosen a market as the global system of economy.

Another distinction that is often made is between the entire economy and the "real" economy. The "real" bit is the actual production of the goods and services that we purchase and consume. The rest, which has grown far more quickly than the real economy in recent decades, is the financial economy. This includes all the financial trading—much of it automated and driven by algorithms—of stocks, bonds, currencies and the like. There is a general feeling that if we could just get back to focusing on the real economy, many of the bad consequences of our current economic system would melt away. I'm sure that the financial markets exacerbate the problems, as through them real prices are affected that serve to hasten the transfer of funds from the poorest to the richest. However, I think that even for the real economy, the market approach is far from ideal.

Throughout human history, there have been many civilisations that have not relied on the market as the underlying method of economy, as David Graeber and David Wengrow explain in their book "The Dawn of Everything". Even when market approaches have emerged, they have not generally become ubiquitous. Rather, the market would fill in some gaps and provide access to exotic luxuries. By contrast, during my lifetime alone, even in the UK, the market has grown to cover more and more areas of our lives.

When I was a child, a great deal of productive work happened outside the market economy. Caring for older people, socialising children, preparing food, cleaning and maintaining clothes and homes, arranging community and cultural celebrations—this all tended to be done for free, in that it was not part of the market and was not mediated by money. It was done mainly by women (and indeed, much of it still is). There were several problems with this. Women had little choice in the matter, and few chances to escape from this work if they were unhappy doing it. These days women are often thought to be in a better position, as they have the choice to go out to work and have fulfilling careers (though in reality, many are forced into undertaking unfulfilling paid labour out of financial necessity). They then have a choice as to how to spend (a large proportion of) their earnings in the marketplace to buy in the services that traditionally they themselves, along with other community members, might have been expected to undertake for free. They can buy child care and care for older relatives, along with convenience foods, labour-saving devices and chemicals that lessen the time needed to run a home (while creating a significant environmental toll). Shared community and cultural events have become fewer (as well as more commercialised), with more of our leisure time being spent in restaurants, clubs, cinemas and escape rooms—all operating, of course, within the market economy.

I'm not suggesting we should go back to a world where women have little choice and no ability to be recognised for their work. Indeed, in today's economic system, it would simply not be possible for most women to be unpaid full-time housekeepers even if they wanted to. A key reason for this is that wages have failed to keep pace with the cost of living.

VALUE BEYOND MONEY

When I was young, a man in a relatively low-waged job could afford to feed, clothe and house a family. Today, that is simply not possible. Even with two wage earners, many families find themselves in poverty. Sometimes we hear voices from older generations saying that the problem is that families these days spend money on modern luxuries that they themselves did without in the past, luxuries like central heating, cars, smartphones, streaming platform subscriptions, fast foods and so on. But the reality is that these things are difficult to avoid, and are strongly advocated in the media. Indeed, if the poorer people didn't buy smartphones, streaming subscriptions and fast foods, we wouldn't have the economic growth that promises jobs for all (not that this promise has ever been delivered). In particular, without smartphones and streaming subscriptions, we wouldn't get all the messaging that encourages us to be good consumers and buy the latest things—of vital importance if the aim is continued market economic growth. As a result of all these increased purchasing demands, more money is needed to run a household, but wages have not kept up. Hence the rise in consumer debt and poverty.

Another problem that has emerged as more women have increasingly become part of the paid workforce is the gender inequality in wages. Some of this is simple patriarchy; men running businesses who hold a belief (or should that read prejudice?) that men (like themselves) are better workers than women, and thus pay men more than women for the same job. They also don't promote women as readily for the same reasons, creating a further dimension to the inequality in wages. But much of the inequity has come about precisely because tasks that were traditionally women's work (and previously outside the market economy) were free in market terms. They didn't cost money. So, when they became part of the market economy, they were priced as cheaply as possible, meaning they were extremely undervalued.

Socialising our children is highly skilled work, and the future of our societies depends on it being done well. All too often this work is now being outsourced to people who are paid the minimum wage, who have little training, and who have no meaningful personal investment in the development of the mini human beings they are being entrusted with. We can see that we're not taking the socialising of our children seriously as a society when we look at the levels of mental ill-health in our young people. Equally, preparing food from fresh ingredients is no longer valued or even seen as possible by many. People have neither the time nor the skills to prepare meals from scratch, and so we rely increasingly on ultra-processed foods and takeaways. We can see that we're under-valuing the importance of feeding our families by the increasing prevalence of diabetes and obesity, and the other health inequalities across the board in our society that just keep growing.

I would argue that marketising areas of work that traditionally fall to women has led directly to them being under-valued by society. If we want to fix that, we need to find a way of taking those areas of work out of the market mechanism.

A Commons Economy

As I said, we need to govern planet Earth as a commons. This requires an economic system that has rules of usage for the planet's resources, which are determined by all those that depend on their use. We need ways of monitoring this usage, and we need sanctions that can be applied when the rules are broken. Instead, we currently have a free-for-all market economy, in which a few powerful people control the majority of the Earth's resources. They are not subject to any rules, let alone rules that all members of the human race have been involved in making. Even if there were rules, there is no effective monitoring that would spot if those rules were being violated and by whom. There are no sanctions for misuse; on the contrary, there are financial rewards for the "best" exploiters of this world's resources. No global authorities, such as the United Nations, recognise that this planet Earth commons exists. Even if they did, they would have no control over either the nation states or the multinational corporations that now privately own the planet's resources.

For me, the ultimate purpose of my work has become to try to help a commons economy to emerge for planet Earth. This urgently needs to take over from our market economy approach. I believe that such a transformation is possible; after all, many transformations in systems of economy have occurred in human history. But I also suspect that it will be a long and difficult process that we may well not have time to complete, given the current polycrisis that is threatening so many of the planet's natural cycles and capacities.

A New Economy?

This brings me on to a wider point about how I would define a new or alternative economy. I feel these terms are frequently used interchangeably and often without much meaning. For me, they do have very distinct meanings, which I'll try to encapsulate here.

Much of the new economy movement is preoccupied with fairer or greener business models—such as cooperatives or B Corps—with some top-down regulation to curb the worst excesses of the market. Local currency and mutual credit projects also fit into this new economy activity, from my perspective. New economy thinking and work tends to focus on three key areas.

The first area is around net zero carbon. Or even better, carbon negativity. This means ensuring that a company's operations don't add CO_2 to the atmosphere, or actually take CO_2 out of the atmosphere. This might be done by the company promising to plant trees somewhere in order to offset the carbon they are emitting. This is highly problematic, with some suggesting that even planting those trees promised so far is not physically possible without causing unintended damage to other ecosystems. There have been scandals about carbon trading schemes that are doing more harm than good, buying up land with great natural ecosystems and digging it up to plant monocultures of trees that are not well suited to the local conditions. As a result, many don't survive to maturity (which is when they are actually absorbing more carbon). Better than offsetting, companies might reduce their carbon footprint by minimising the carbon used in their operations and through their supply chains (known as "insetting"). For example, a factory might change its lighting to LED bulbs, thereby reducing its CO_2 emissions.

When measuring their carbon footprint, companies and local authorities tend to focus on their scope one and scope two emissions. Scope one emissions are the emissions they are directly responsible for, such as from the petrol or diesel they put into their own vehicles, or the gas they burn in their boilers for heating. They can cut this by, for example, switching to electric vehicles or using a heat pump instead of a boiler. Scope two emissions are from the electricity they buy in. They can cut that by choosing more efficient products (like LED bulbs), and by ensuring that they buy electricity only from a renewable energy provider (although if you're using electricity from the grid, you can't really trace units of power back to their production). But to have a full picture of CO_2 emissions, companies need to think about their scope three emissions too. These are the emissions from the production and transportation of all the things the company buys in. When a company is replacing its fleet of vehicles with electric ones to reduce its scope one emissions, it might well inadvertently increase its scope three emissions.

But even if companies try to address their scope three emissions, in reality, most CO_2 calculations don't take the full product lifecycle into account. What about the fact that to sell my zero-carbon widgets, I am reliant on shops and warehouses, which all have lighting and heating? I'm reliant on customers travelling to shops, or on delivery vehicles travelling to customers, and I have no control over how those journeys are being fuelled. What about the electricity that my power-driven widgets consume in their day-to-day use? What about the customers driving to a waste disposal facility to recycle my widgets, or the rubbish truck that picks up my used widgets from people's homes? What about all the businesses involved in the supply chain that enable me to make my widgets? The heavy machinery used to extract the raw materials it is made from, and the transport that gets the people who operate that machinery to work every day? If most businesses truly wanted to not be responsible for their carbon emissions, they would just shut up shop. Let's just say that no amount of new economy thinking on the part of companies or activists is going to be truly transformative. The only thing that can actually halt anthropogenic carbon emissions is if we outlaw the extraction of fossil fuels at a global level. Rather than fit flow restrictors at the ends of the hoses, which only encourages the development of new hoses to take the flow, we need to turn off the mains tap. Clearly, we can't do that instantly; a great deal of planning is needed to ensure that the gradual switching off of the tap happens without creating dreadful consequences for humanity.

A second focus for the new economy is the development of a more circular economy. Our ever-growing market economy demands obsolescence, so that there is a reason to keep producing more new stuff. We extract materials, produce things, use them for a bit, and then discard them. It is a linear process of take, make, use and lose. The resource footprint to supply this market economic system is growing exponentially, as is the level of waste products and pollution of land, water and air that it creates. The idea of the circular economy is that we will use the waste products to create the inputs for the next products. Natural systems do this constantly, so surely we can emulate nature and do the same?

Of course, I'm in favour of trying to circularise our economy. Mending and repairing things to extend their life should reduce the need to purchase new things. Lending and borrowing equipment and clothes, buying second hand wherever possible, and recycling our waste into component parts that can then be recombined to form new products—these are clearly good things to do and can limit our personal resource footprints.

However, at a global scale, our ability to extract pollutants from air, water and land at a molecular level is very limited. And even the easier task of sorting our waste and deconstructing complex products is not really working despite the huge efforts that have been made in recent decades. Each time I look in a recycling box or bin, it is clear that most people have no idea of the complexity of deconstruction and sorting that is required for recycling to be possible. Meanwhile, we hear of waste sorted for recycling being mixed with general rubbish when it is collected, or see footage on the news of waste supposedly for recycling ending up on beaches in distant places. This happens because the market has failed in the area of recycling, making it impossible to create profitable businesses to handle all the waste.

Meanwhile, we keep developing novel materials that perform better than older materials (say for storing and conducting electricity, or for resilience and strength). We keep inventing new tools such as smartphones, electric vehicles and MRI scanners. These all require new minerals to be extracted, and so the cycle of increasing extraction continues. Some think that economic growth and new technology is the way to resolve our social and environmental problems, a concept known as "green growth". But as I see it, a totally circular economy will never be possible, regardless of all the efforts being made within the new economy movement. Therefore, green growth is a myth.

A third area of effort that is core to new economy thinking is social justice. This is basically a socialist approach, aiming to redistribute wealth away from the investors and towards the workers. Pay policies that limit the earnings of CEOs to a factor of the lowest paid workers within a business are an example of this thinking playing out. Another is the creation of cooperatives, in which workers, customers or suppliers (and sometimes all three) strive for a fairer sharing of profits, alongside shared decision making. Initiatives like the Bristol Pound and mutual credit, that aim to make the financial system work better for the smaller players, are further examples. Again, I'm very pleased this work is happening. It's absolutely vital to do what we can to rebuild some equality and equity in our distribution of resources. However, this work still fits within a market approach. Paying people fairly for their work, and ensuring everyone has access to decent work to enable them to live within the current system—these things still need businesses to be growing and creating jobs for an ever-increasing population. Growth is thus still built into the thinking. Cooperatives are businesses at the end of the day, needing to make profits by adding value, keen to expand their remit, since growth is the main mark of success for any business. A fairer economy that is founded on jobs and growth can only ever be a temporary solution in a finite world.

All aspects of the new economy movement are of course vital for qualitatively improving the current market economy. But they are still firmly rooted within the current system. They are based on the assumption that the economy is all about businesses, trade and money. A market-based economy is by definition about businesses "adding value", which is a synonym for extracting financial value from customers. It is always about growth. So as I've said, I'm very pleased that lots of people are working hard on new economy ideas to improve the current market economy. Hopefully, they will buy us sufficient time to do the transformative work of designing an alternative economy. For that is what we need: a truly alternative economic system that is not based on markets, on businesses, or on private ownership of land, and which is not mediated by money. Sadly, as yet, not many people are working on alternative economics.

An Alternative Economy: A Commons Economy

I'm trying to imagine a totally different economic system: a commons economy. What would be the key features of such an economy? Would it need any kind of metrics or currency to operate?

There is a problem of scale to be addressed here. The commons we're familiar with are generally fairly small, and the usership well within the "Dunbar" number (a number postulated by Robin Dunbar that is related to the number of social relationships we can maintain), generally put at about 150 people. At such a level, a tally is not needed. If a member of the group keeps misbehaving and letting the community down, it will be spotted, without any need for formal metrics. A currency is not needed; I know who I'm obligated to and who "owes" me one. I know who is dependent on the community because of illness or disability. I have a sense of fairness and a feeling of care for everyone in the group. The sanctions are also fairly easy to understand, since the community will all recognise a miscreant and shun them. At a global scale, it's much harder to spot who is doing the damage, and very hard to completely exclude them. By definition, unless we resort to capital punishment, all living beings remain part of the commons. We therefore need to have some metrics to spot when things are going wrong. We need some currencies so we can monitor who is extracting or degrading value. We need to devise sanctions and limit autonomy when individuals are bent on abusing the commons.

We generally think of the word "currency" as being linked solely to money. I now have a different understanding of "currency" thanks to the Metacurrency Project and the work of Arthur Brock. Their work introduced me to the concept of "current-sees": things that make visible the flow of non-financial value. A commons economy definitely needs current-sees, so that we can see the movement, accumulation, and depletion of non-financial assets. Financial currencies mediate the flow of financial value through market transactions. By contrast, current-sees make the movements of real value visible, rather than mediate those movements through transactions.

Some pages back, I was wondering how we could measure gratitude as a proxy for the awareness of mutual interdependence that is vital for social cohesion. As I pointed out, measuring purchases of flowers and boxes of chocolates is not going to do the job. That measures the market activity, not the actual instance of gratitude. If we could somehow count instances of gratitude using a current-see, and observe the metrics of that current-see change over time, we would be aware when and where social cohesion was waxing and waning.

VALUE BEYOND MONEY

We could see who was not recognising their place within the web of human co-dependency. We could then take action in some way to bring that person back into the fold, perhaps by making it clear to them that they can only survive thanks to the care they receive from their wider community, challenging their egotistic illusions through experiential learning of the reality of mutual interdependence and the power of love.

Whereas financial currencies are fungible or interchangeable, reducing all values to a monetary value, current-sees are not at all fungible. I can state my bank balance in US Dollars if necessary. But no amount of gratitude is equivalent to an amount of clean air, and there can be no exchange rate for biodiversity against social cohesion. With money, we can compare apples and pears in market terms. With current-sees, we cannot compare any one value with any other value.

In the financial economic system, there is one form of capital: money. In a commons system, we can recognise many distinct forms of capital. How many distinct types of capital should be recognised is up for grabs. I've seen systems describing ten, framed as if these were absolute. I would suggest that, like the colours in the rainbow, how we separate them and how many of them we differentiate depends on our language and conceptual framing. In coming to a global understanding of the assets we need to count in order for a global commons to function, we'll need to consider different cultural, philosophical, and scientific understandings of what is important when trying to safeguard the future resources of planet Earth and to create an equitable and peaceful global society. That said, I'll attempt to split up the types of capital in my own way, as a start.

First and foremost, there are environmental capitals. The most obvious of these is the land. We need to develop some kind of land use framework to ensure all the functions of the land are represented. We have to have some way of deciding what land can be for human needs (such as agriculture, built environment and transport routes), and what land must be reserved for nature. It is natural land that provides habitat for the diversity of life on Earth, in turn providing "ecosystem services". Arguably, this is still about meeting human needs; ecosystem-services process the pollution and waste that we generate. Soil quality should perhaps be seen as a capital in its own right, as without healthy soil rich in living organisms, our ability to grow food sustainably is limited. With the rate of soil loss through poor land management and erosion, and with its increasing sterilisation caused by industrial fertilisers, pesticides and herbicides, the United Nations suggested in 2019 that we may only have sixty harvests left, though that number is disputed and varies from place to place. Also within environmental capitals are the capitals of clean air, freshwater and oceans. Within each of these, we could again look at the various uses we make of them, and the resources that are left for nature. Alternatively, we might be able to avoid making so many distinctions between these capitals if we just used biodiversity as a marker instead—within soil, air, saltwater and freshwater. The more biodiversity there is in each system, the more the land, air and water are processed by different life forms, improving the balance of different nutrients through natural cycles. It is through biodiversity that the "ecosystem services" that neutralise our waste can happen, as long as we don't overwhelm nature.

VALUE BEYOND MONEY

As an example of how a land-based current-see might work even within our existing economic system, consider this: there is software that can grade satellite images of the Earth pixel by pixel, determining whether each pixel is natural forest, forest managed for lumber, agricultural land or built environment. We can imagine the pixels being scored to give an overall environmental value of planet Earth's land, split by national boundaries perhaps (as a stepping stone to my envisaged global commons economy future), and by land ownership (again, as an interim step). We would be able to see and count the depletion of environmental land capital value and assign responsibility to land owners and governments. We'd also be able to see where regenerative work is being effective, so that we could learn lessons from each other and replicate good practice. We would be trying to increase the score. We do seem driven as humans to increase our scores. It is just so unfortunate that we've chosen Gross Domestic Product (GDP) as the one we're trying to increase in our current system. Increasing environmental land value, or the value of any of the multiple capitals (apart from financial capital) is not a problem, because these are scores of quality, not quantity.

In 2020, the UK government commissioned Sir Partha Dasgupta to look into the economics of biodiversity. The resulting report, published in January 2021, came to some similar conclusions to my own, albeit from a mainstream perspective. In effect, Sir Partha found that nature is not accounted for in market economic transactions. Nobody is doing the bookkeeping for the asset register of planet Earth, and that needs to change. The value of nature itself needs to be accounted for. Sir Partha doesn't quite get as far as a solution for how this could be done. He assumes the valuation of nature will be in financial terms, but, reading the review, I think that if he had come across the concept of current-sees, he might have proposed a current-see rather than a financial valuation.

Second, we have social capitals. These are basically capitals to do with human life. Again, they need to be split down into some component parts. Human health equality is a key one. Recognising where in the world human health is being negatively affected by toxins in our environment is vital, as is understanding where there is access to clean water and sanitation. On the other hand, access to advanced medicines, for example to treat cancer, is not a valid metric, at least not initially. We need to level up before we focus on the expectations of the richest people in the world. We also need to consider the diseases of affluence—type two diabetes and obesity—which are in large part caused by the ultra-processed foods that are marketed to us to grow the multinational companies that produce them. There are already metrics that we could call current-sees for global health; datasets of infant mortality, and of the incidence and prevalence of non-communicable diseases. We just don't give these metrics enough importance, and we don't have a shared goal of improving health inequalities at a global scale. At best, these datasets are used to justify the efforts of big pharmaceutical companies to create and sell more drugs. "Big pharma" cannot be trusted to have our best interests at heart, because like all businesses, their primary purpose is to increase their profits, not to address health inequalities.

Human wellbeing and mental health also need to be a current-see. It seems likely that data from such a current-see would enable us to see links emerging in the data between poor mental health and damage to the human spirit through participation in meaningless work, the fragmentation of communities and culture, and the loss of spiritual connection with nature and all that is (which some people might perhaps call God). Community cohesion would be another capital, with current-sees perhaps being the incidence of violence, the level of care shown to the most vulnerable members of the community, and the amount of gratitude as an acknowledgement that we are all reliant on each other.

Knowledge could be split from the other social capitals. Knowledge itself is perhaps too vague a term to encompass access to shared learning, opportunities for creativity, and the extent to which we are resilient and adaptable. Without these human attributes we will be unable to survive. At the moment knowledge is often not shared, because of commercial concerns. We have intellectual property laws that seek to enable people to make profits at others' expense thanks to having a novel idea—an idea that they would not have had without the education and myriad life experiences that led them to the point where they had their novel thought. Our schools, meanwhile, downplay creativity and adaptability, as currently the main aim of much education is seemingly to fit people for the workforce of a market economy. It's really hard to know how we could create current-sees for creativity and knowledge sharing, but we need to think about it.

Finally, we have manufactured capital. In our current system, once a thing is produced and sold, it has no ongoing value. It only adds to GDP through its production and sale. But as part of a move to a fully circular economy, we must care for and maintain our manufactured capital. Not to do so is highly wasteful of all the resources and effort that went into making it. What we need to count in a manufactured capital current-see is not an ever-growing number of manufactured things. Rather, we need to count the longevity of manufactured items. This would start to focus us on maintenance and repair as the valuable activities they are.

The idea of current-sees is thus to count the actual things that are of value in creating and maintaining a global commons, rather than counting money as if, of itself, it were a thing of value, which it is not.

Money is not the only thing that is unique to a market economy approach. There are other building blocks to the economic system that would need to change in a commons economy. Two especially: land ownership and corporations.

Private land ownership simply cannot exist in a global commons. Any use of the worlds' resources must be in accordance with the rules of usage set out by the commons governance. There would be no exclusive rights to any particular area of land (or sea). Where a need has been identified for a highly controlled activity to take place in a specific location, rules would ensure that only those who have the training and knowledge can be involved.

Specific groups of people with clear purposes, which I'll call organisations, can also be recognised by the commons framework. Organisations would be needed to facilitate the production of highly technical products (like computers and vehicles) that rely on the manufacture of component parts using materials from around the globe. Organisations would also be needed to enable the delivery of coordinated specialised services, such as within healthcare.

These commons organisations would not be the same as corporations in a market economy. There are two clear differences. First, apart from non-profit organisations, corporations in the market economy have a purpose above that which you might assume from their activities; their main objective is to create a return on investment for their shareholders. In a commons economy, there is no trade, and therefore no profit. The concept of investment would not really exist. Effort and resources would be needed to start a new project, of course, but these would be assigned by the commons' governance system. The sole purpose of an organisation in a commons economy would be its activity, undertaken for the common good with consent, as determined by a democratic decision-making process, operating completely unlike our current political system (i.e. not party based, and not mediated by elected representatives). The entire commons economy would be purpose-driven.

The second difference between organisations in a commons economy and corporations in a market economy would be that people within the organisation share the responsibility for undertaking its activities. The opposite is true of corporations in a market economy. The corporation itself is considered a "person" in the eyes of the law, and any fines or penalties are usually levied against the company itself. True, directors are sometimes prosecuted for the failings of their company to abide by the law, but rarely. Rather, they tend to shift any blame to the least powerful people within the company, sacking operators or middle managers as part of clearing themselves of any blame. A dreadful example would be the Union Carbide disaster in Bhopal. The company paid the fines, local staff were largely blamed, and the directors were not incarcerated for the immense loss of life and severe illness caused by their company's actions. The operators and middle managers were in reality probably only doing what the company implicitly asked them to do, which was to hang their morals on the hook along with their coats when they came to work each day, to cut corners and to put gain first every time.

Tokens in Bristol Pay

Bristol Pay was never going to be able to create a global commons economy on its own. However, we need to think about the journey humankind will have to undertake in order to view the economy differently. Rupert Read has developed the term "thrutopia"—the process of trying to create a better system. It's not enough to imagine utopias; we have to imagine the baby steps that can take us from where we are on the journey towards the utopia we seek. We need several people to try different paths, all heading towards the same destination. Some paths will work, others not. The milestones along the way won't really be known until we've passed them. As we travel, our ideas about the final destination will develop and be honed. But for this to occur, we have to start the journey. I saw Bristol Pay tokens as a small step on a possible path, through which we could offer people a way to learn experientially about values other than money, about areas of life that could operate outside a market, and about the impact we can make towards shared goals by working together. The tokens would be experiments in current-sees,

VALUE BEYOND MONEY

through which we could learn more about how current-sees could be effective in coordinating our efforts. Whilst Bristol Pay couldn't create a global commons, it could experiment with some of the building blocks that are necessary to create a global commons, and this would be important work.

Behaviour Change

It was at this time, with a growing awareness that a market was not necessarily the best or only approach to organising an economy, that our thinking moved away from the tokens being earned and spent. Instead, we saw that different sorts of tokens might be assigned in different ways, and that most would not be spent at all.

This might seem strange. We live in a society where the only reason to accumulate our main token—money—is to spend it. Indeed, we think that everything needs to be incentivised (a word that barely existed before 1970) by money. Companies believe people will work harder if that will enable them to earn more money. Shop owners reason that customers will be loyal if they get a little financial kickback each time they spend money at their store. Governments think that people might change their car if doing so will save them money in car tax. It's not just about carrots, it's about sticks too. Local authorities think that the threat of a fine is the thing that will encourage dog owners to pick up their dog's poo.

But there is evidence to suggest that financial incentives and penalties, often referred to as nudge economics, are not as influential as we might imagine in changing behaviours. There are even some studies that show that in the long term, some incentives may decrease the intended behaviour.

Dan Ariely, a professor in psychology and behavioural economics, and James Heyman, an economist and mathematician, looked at why this might be. They carried out an experiment getting three cohorts of people to complete a meaningless task on a computer. One cohort was told that the research was really important, but that unfortunately it was unfunded, so participants couldn't be paid for their time. The second was told that funding was very limited, but that they would receive a nominal fifty cents to thank them for their time. The third set were told that the research was properly funded and that they'd be paid a living wage equivalent for the time the task took, equating to five dollars. The researchers then looked at how much effort the participants had put into the task. They found that those doing it for free and those doing it for a market wage worked pretty hard. However, those doing it for (a frankly derisory) fifty cents put in very little effort. They then repeated the experiment but with slightly different conditions in terms of the rewards: one cohort were to receive nothing, the second were to receive a Snickers bar (worth about fifty cents at the time), and the third were to receive a box of chocolates (worth about five dollars). It is important to emphasise that they didn't mention the value of the gifts that would be provided; they just said they were gifts to thank them for their participation. When they looked at how hard the participants worked, they found they all put in similar amounts of effort not unlike the hard workers in the first experiment. They then repeated the experiment a third time, using the same rewards as in the second experiment, but telling the participants the financial value of the gifts. They repeated the results of the first run of the experiment.

VALUE BEYOND MONEY

Unsurprisingly, the people who knew they were receiving a reward that undervalued their time did not put in much effort.

What the researchers found is that as soon as things are framed in financial terms, a market mentality is triggered. When people are taking part as volunteers in a social economy, even if a thank you gift is being received, they engage fully in the experiment and work hard. When they are being rewarded fairly in market terms, they also work hard. But when they see themselves as being undervalued within a market economy, they are not prepared to put in much effort.

Government incentives never value people's efforts at a market rate. To do so would be excessively expensive. But as a result, the incentives they offer are doomed to fail in their aim of changing behaviour.

There are other explanations for what underpins our behaviours. The one I've come across that makes most sense to me is called the Individual Social Material (ISM) model, developed by Andrew Darnton, which is based on Dale Southerton's international review of behaviour change initiatives. The ISM model says that there are three main dimensions that determine our behaviour, and suggests a methodology for organisations and authorities to use with communities to change behaviours.

The first dimension is our individual nature; what we think about ourselves based on the roles we have in our society. For example, I might see myself as being a white middle-class woman living in the UK. I have various expectations based on this identity; for instance, that I will eat in restaurants occasionally. I have routines that seem appropriate to my identity, such as eating muesli for breakfast and doing laundry using my washing machine. I have work skills, such as bookkeeping, and some skills that I use in my leisure time (itself a concept that I have thanks to my identity), including dancing and singing. I'm a mother, a daughter and a sister, as well as an aunt and a great aunt. These roles and beliefs determine a lot about how I think and behave. They help to create my personal value system and morals.

The second dimension is our social nature. I want to behave in ways that are accepted by my peers and community. I want people to like me and to approve of my choices. I don't want to stick out like a sore thumb or antagonise people. As a result, I modify my behaviour every day. I don't want to seem greedy or selfish, but to appear well-informed and thoughtful. The different groups I'm part of require slightly different behaviours and approaches, and I sometimes feel I'm a bit of a chameleon as a result. What is appropriate in the social dancing I do (namely very close physical contact and some harmless flirtation) is not at all appropriate in choir practice or at work, where some might see me as somewhat reserved.

The third dimension is the material situation that we find ourselves in. This describes what is possible within my society. For example, my moral feelings about my duty to care for the planet might mean that I want to cycle. But if there is no safe cycling route, that would curtail my cycling behaviour. I might feel strongly that public transport should be free. But riding trains and buses without paying is not possible without facing sanctions; the law can thus also curtail my behaviour.

Here's the thing. Let's say we want to encourage people to use public transport instead of personal motorised vehicles. This is important if we are to reduce our material footprint (even if truly net zero carbon cars were possible). Let's say we want to encourage a wealthy corporate lawyer to change their behaviour. At the moment, this lawyer is driving around in a Tesla. They are perhaps thinking from an individual perspective, "I am a successful lawyer, and I need a mode of transport that fits in with my understanding of my status. I enjoy driving around in my Tesla and I've earned it. Buses are for losers." They might be thinking from a social perspective, "My Tesla looks great on the driveway! My neighbours can see that I'm both successful and that I care about the environment. When I show up at a meeting and say to clients that I'm sorry I'm a few minutes late because I couldn't find anywhere to charge my Tesla, they are instantly impressed." From a material perspective, there are plenty of Tesla cars for sale at an affordable price for this lawyer, and a growing number of places where the Tesla can be charged, including in their garage at home.

There are lots of things that need to change before the lawyer will change their mode of transport. Yes, a decent public transport system is one of them, but frankly this lawyer isn't even going to look at the bus and train options unless their individual and social perspectives change. This lawyer needs to be thinking, "When I show up at a meeting and say that I'm sorry I'm late because the number 42 bus was delayed, everyone will think I'm really cool for taking public transport. My neighbours would think I was rather selfish and egotistical if I had a private vehicle parked on the driveway, even if it was electric." Further, they need to be thinking, "I'm a member of the human race and I share in the responsibility for looking after this planet. I don't want to have more than my fair share of resources. I would feel bad about using a private vehicle to get around every day."

The ISM model of behaviour makes it clear just how difficult changing behaviour is. We have to start with changing how people see themselves, both as individuals and in relation to others.

The problem of changing people's behaviour is especially acute at the start of the process. Not many people are prepared to be one of the eccentrics who kickstart new ways of behaving. Many years ago, one of my daughters was talking to me about an attractive man they'd met who had a "man-bun". This was not a thing I'd come across. Men sometimes had long hair in my social circle, and some even tied it up in a ponytail. But a bun? That was seen as a feminine hairstyle at the time. Of course, in the intervening years, man-buns have become common. And why not? They are very practical—more so than ponytails—especially for sports and in hot weather. Interestingly, bunches, side-buns (also known as space-buns), and side plaits are still reserved for females, generally. I look forward to noticing a few brave men sporting side-buns and the trend catching on at some point.

It seems there are tipping points at which a behaviour changes from being highly eccentric or weird, to being avant-garde or chic (but only seen as appropriate for a specific minority, say pop stars), to being completely normal. If we want new ways of thinking and behaving to emerge, we need to understand how to create those tipping points.

These days, influencers on social media platforms are often credited with setting new trends. However, some research has shown that the best way to create a new trend is to focus on minority groups first. Let's say I'm part of a close-knit group of people who are already seen as somewhat apart from the mainstream, living in a small intentional community of about fifty people, focused on spirituality and connection. If I try something new in that community, I can feel fairly safe that I will still be accepted. The people around me will notice I'm doing something new and will ask me about it. A couple of friends might think it's cool and join me in my new behaviour. If just five people start doing whatever it is, that's 10% of the group. The new behaviour is now not completely eccentric and wacky, but a viable alternative to the mainstream within that group. Then more people catch on. The tipping point for "normal", according to various pieces of research, is somewhere between 18% and 25%, which in this scenario is only 9 to 13 people, and is likely to be achieved quite easily. Meanwhile, the people in my community interact with the wider community too. Thus, the new behaviour, already normalised within the group, becomes visible as a minority activity in the mainstream.

The first task of delivering behaviour change therefore seems to be to create little minorities where new behaviours can be experimented with safely, without risk of ridicule by the mainstream. A norm can then be established within each minority group, which subsequently influences the wider society. We can see this process at work through cultural appropriation of minority behaviours and fashions by members of the majority culture. An example might be white people sporting dreadlocks. This is often called out as a bad thing by those from within the minority cultures who see themselves as having ownership of that behaviour, especially when the cultural or spiritual relevance of the behaviour is not understood by those appropriating it. But regardless, it is evidence of the effectiveness of minorities in spreading changes in behaviour.

Applied Tokenomics

The Bristol Pay tokens seemed to offer the potential of creating minorities who would be willing to change their behaviours. The tokens would not confer any reward beyond the token itself. The recognition that a positive action had been taken would be the only reward. In this way, we could build on learnings from Dan Ariely and James Heyman's work, and combine their non-market approach to reward with an ISM understanding of behaviour change.

This might all sound highly academic and theoretical. Are there any real-world applications of this approach that suggest it could work? The answer is that there are loads of examples all around us, and the last decade has shown us all just how powerful the approach is.

Take social media. We can think of Facebook, Instagram, TikTok and the like as ways of influencing our individual and social behavioural drivers, helping us define ourselves and building a concept of our social standing. Sadly, the behaviours these platforms influence us towards are mainly to increase our consumption of various things, including social media itself, but that is because of the business model behind them, rather than being an inherent feature of the technology. These platforms are built as marketing platforms, through which we are fed content that is likely to keep us scrolling, in turn increasing the number of adverts

VALUE BEYOND MONEY

and the amount of paid content we are subjected to. When using social media platforms, the main way we get feedback on our social standing is through various types of current-see, such as impressions, likes, shares, and comments. Arguably, these current-sees have become too meaningful in many people's lives, such that one of the main motivations for doing something becomes, for some people, to create content for their social media profile. Worse, for a significant proportion of users, the activity they've posted about loses its value for them if other people don't endorse it in some way. Thus, many people are concerned that the use of social media is causing increased anxiety and feelings of low self-worth, particularly amongst young people. But whilst our current forms of market-driven social media may well be doing more harm than good, there is the potential to create a different sort of social media based on goals other than increasing consumption. If the aim of the platforms were not to make us avid consumers but rather to encourage us to collaborate and share positive ideas, their functioning and governance would be completely different.

Fitbits are another example of behaviour change being modified by current-sees. Having a goal for the number of steps you take each day and seeing how you're doing against that goal turns out to be a powerful motivator for many people. Meanwhile, you might find yourself comparing your performance with friends and family members. In this way, Fitbits, too, work at both an individual and a social level to change behaviour, this time in a positive way.

Duolingo is a language learning app. Like a Fitbit, Duolingo is highly gamified, with a whole range of points to drive engagement, and the ability to follow friends and give them a "high five" for doing well. There are some points that you can't spend, which just count how many exercises you've done. There are others that you can spend within the app, for example buying you more time on time-limited exercises, or maintaining your running streak if you miss a day of practice. There are also league tables to keep you engaged if you like an element of competition. These are all slightly different current-sees, measuring the value of your language learning work in slightly different ways to maximise the chance that one of these metrics will hook you.

Of course, nobody expects to be able to get 50p off their latte or tea with their Fitbit steps, social media likes, or Duolingo "lingots". The current-see itself is what motivates, not its ability to confer purchasing power in the market economy. Sometimes a current-see can confer rewards within the platform or game, but generally not. These current-sees are a reward in their own right. They are not a means of buying things outside the app. The reason they are meaningful to us is that they show how we are doing against our personal goals (individual motivation) and in terms of our social reputation (social motivation).

However, powerful though Fitbits and Duolingo have been in changing individuals' behaviours, I feel they've missed a trick. You can only get a feeling for how many people are using Duolingo and how well you're doing in the grand scheme of language learning if you use Duolingo yourself. Other people have no idea that language learning is becoming a fun thing to do. We also can't say that 2,500 people in Bristol are learning a foreign language on Duolingo. Nor can we say that 400 people in Bristol have become proficient in a foreign language within the last year after starting as complete beginners. We have no idea what those statistics would be. Duolingo has that data and could tell us. Indeed, occasionally Duolingo does share some statistics that it thinks will interest us, such as that more people are learning a foreign language through Duolingo than in the school system in the USA. But current-sees only reach their full potential to change behaviour when large numbers of people can see them. This is where we saw the possibilities for gamified current-sees in Bristol having a real impact. By changing behaviours at an in-group level and being able to tell a story with the current-sees about the numbers of people involved (not the individuals), we could start to move those behaviours from being solely within an in-group to being cool in the mainstream, and, in due course, as the number of tokens in a particular current-see increases, to reach the tipping point for the new behaviour to become a social norm.

This seemed like a breakthrough. Going back to the problem of how to grow social movements, we already knew how difficult it is for new ideas to catch on, especially if they are linked to an ideology that separates an in-group from the wider society. However, if we can create changes that are not linked to an ideology but rather are seen as games, and if we use current-sees to share a narrative around behaviour change that encourages others to get on board, then we have the potential to shift behaviour in the mainstream.

Let's compare this with the ability of social media to create environmentally positive changes in behaviour. If anyone is foolhardy enough to state on social media that they are being green, they will immediately be trolled by several accounts who will call them out as hypocrites, pointing out their numerous failings (driving a car, flying to a far-off country, eating a hamburger, etc). If instead the focus is on counting specific positive actions, these cannot be undermined in the same way.

Unlike social credit systems described in dystopian science fiction, the Bristol Pay current-sees would only count positive actions. Failures, where we don't live up to our high standards, would not be counted. We can always pull up our socks and try again. Tomorrow is another day, and spending time feeling like we've failed (so we might as well not bother at all) is only damaging to the positive effort.

One last point on all this. Too often, as individuals, we feel apathetic when considering the tiny amount of difference our actions make. What is the point of not driving my car to the supermarket today when we are told that some of the largest countries in the world are increasing their fossil fuel consumption daily? But by having a current-see, we can see that our efforts do count, that we are part of a bigger story; that every little helps. We need to move away from apathy and despair and towards collaboration and celebration if we are to stand a chance of making widespread changes to behaviour in the mainstream.

Thanks Tokens

In the summer of 2021, we were trying to design some tokens for Bristol Pay. To sum up our thinking, the idea was that the tokens would deliver some kind of impact as an add-on to the payment system. The tokens would act as current-sees to help us visualise non-financial value. The payment system would be the way we attracted people onto the platform with a value proposition they could understand (namely, raising money for voluntary sector services). Once they were there, we'd encourage them to engage with the tokens by making them feel like a game.

The first idea we had was a Thanks token. This would potentially have several impacts, such as reducing isolation and building social cohesion. People joining the challenge would be given a universal basic income (UBI) of Thanks tokens, being topped up to, say, ten at the start of every day. There would be two aspects to the game. One aspect would be that you would get positive messages to reinforce your thanking behaviour. The aim would be to encourage you to give away your Thanks tokens every day, either to specific people on the platform that you had chosen to connect to (a neighbour who did you a favour, for example), or to a general pot for people of Bristol (to recognise a random act of kindness by someone not known to you personally). The system could keep a running score of how many Thanks you had given away.

The other aspect would be feeling good about receiving Thanks. Again, the system could count how many Thanks you'd received.

Thinking about the protocols for the digital token design, each Thanks token could only be passed on once. In this way, each gifted token would recognise one act of kindness. A word or two could be added to give some context or description of the act of kindness being rewarded. Toby Harris, our artistic designer, felt such a description would add *"spicy metadata"* that would help to create engaging infographics and visuals for the current-see. Thus, on the website for the tokens, accessible to anyone whether or not they had an account, you might be able to pull data for how many Thanks had been given in Bristol this month compared to last month, and see two graphics. The overall size of the graphic would relate to how many Thanks had been given, but, within that, there might be plants, paint brushes or bags of shopping, again of different sizes, suggesting the relative split between the different sorts of favours for which people were being thanked.

Similarly, an individual user's profile on the app would change depending on the numbers of various tokens held. If you had received lots of Thanks tokens, part of your profile would have a little crowd of people, smiling and waving at you. If you had been collecting, say, cycling tokens, you might have a picture of a bike that gradually got fancier as you did more cycling.

Another aspect of the token protocol would be that tokens could degrade over time. This would mean that if you wanted to maintain your level of Thanks (or other) tokens received, you couldn't rest on your laurels; you would have to keep doing lovely things for people to keep your level high. If you didn't, the little crowd of people on your profile would look less happy and would gradually decrease in number, or in the case of cycling tokens, your bike would get rusty and fall over.

The Thanks token idea might sound similar to a LETS, described in Chapter One. In a LETS, people offer goods and services in exchange for some kind of token, and use those tokens to purchase other goods and services, usually in a hyperlocal scheme. Both approaches aim to encourage an informal meeting of needs through social cohesion. However, Thanks tokens are different from a LETS in a key respect: they are not part of a market approach. With a LETS, the mechanism is to earn and spend, and there is a market, albeit controlled in some respects, that determines what you can buy with your LETS tokens. That is not the case with Thanks tokens. This is important in two key ways. First, if you are incapacitated—such that you have no skills or goods to sell—you can still participate in Thanks because of the UBI daily top up. Second, the scheme will not need to end just because some people have very popular skills whilst others have few opportunities to share their skills.

Volunteering Tokens

A volunteering or participation token would be similar in some respects to the Thanks token. However, rather than be awarded by a UBI, Volunteer tokens would be awarded by groups or organisations, who in turn would have the ability to create tokens on demand. Once again, each token would recognise just one action, and could not be further passed on once awarded. Like Thanks tokens, they would degrade over time, so that to maintain a level of recognised volunteering, you'd need to keep doing it.

As with Thanks tokens, the purpose of the Volunteering token would be to create social cohesion and encourage people to help their communities. Volunteering tokens could assist in meeting low level social needs in the community that would otherwise require input from social services.

This might sound similar to the Hull Coin and Citizen Coin projects developed by Peter Kemp. There are some key differences, however. In the case of Hull Coin and Citizen Coin, the tokens awarded for volunteering or participating in community events can be accepted in return for discounts by participating businesses. The idea is that you get some kind of extrinsic reward that incentivises you to keep volunteering, whilst local businesses can show their appreciation of people's efforts by giving them a discount or special offer. The token cannot be used to pay for things by the businesses; they have no value to them other than helping to drive footfall, for which they are prepared to give a discount.

Many people suggested our Volunteering tokens should work the same way, but I was keen to keep our tokens completely separate from the market economy. On the one hand, I was mindful of the learnings from Dan Ariely and James Heyman's experiments, and the risk that a small reward might actually undermine the volunteering motive rather than increase it. On the other hand, I was not wanting to encourage yet more consumerism. This is because if we want to bring our consumption in line with the carrying capacity of planet Earth, we need less production and consumption, not more. We need the opposite of growth in GDP. In fact, we need to find a way of shrinking our production and consumption without creating negative impacts on human wellbeing. This concept is generally called degrowth. But perhaps more than both of these, I wanted to keep the current-sees completely separate from any kind of market currency so that we could learn more about how they might work in creating impact through collaboration.

Badges

Badges are really a whole range of tokens, not just one. You can think of them like guide or scout badges, where a skill is recognised by a badge sewn onto the child's uniform. The possibilities are endless for the badges we could have. There could also be levels of badges for some skills, such that, assuming you agreed to this sharing of data, if you had achieved expert level in a particular skill, you could train others.

What sorts of skills would we want to recognise? The first category might be the skills that are needed to reduce an individual's resource footprint. These might include the ability to cook using seasonal vegetables from scratch. This skill is largely lacking, even amongst people who have reasonable cooking skills. For many people, cooking involves thinking of a dish first, then buying the ingredients, whether or not these are in season locally. This was me too, until I took the plunge and decided to rely on a local organic veg box for the majority of my produce. Over the course of the intervening years, I have gradually learned how I can make the seemingly endless winter veg boxes (with their repetitive small selection of produce) into a diverse range of soups, stews, curries and stir fries, using herbs and spices from different cuisines to avoid my meals becoming boring. I wish someone had been able to shortcut that learning for me with a couple of lessons.

Various sorts of crafts and technical skills would also merit badges, especially where these can enable us to mend things. Sharing knowledge on how to repair clothes, furniture and appliances would be great starting points.

When XR were working out how they could keep their protests peaceful and avoid arguments with people who were negatively impacted by their actions, they had the great idea of ensuring that everyone who joined them should have de-escalation training. This would equip activists with the soft skills to take the heat out of potential conflicts. When I first heard about this training, I was really excited. Everyone would benefit from learning how to calm arguments in everyday life. But more than that, imagine if 20% of people had completed de-escalation training, how many fights and injuries could be avoided thanks to people having the confidence to step in and calm things down. The resulting reduction in police call-outs, arrests and trips to accident and emergency would save valuable resources, and the overall effect would be to increase social cohesion.

We could also use badges to show moral choices we have made, or celebrate milestones we've achieved. For example, we could pledge to give up using chemicals such as RoundUp in our gardens and thus get a Nature-friendly Gardener badge. Equally, we could get a token for each square metre of lawn (fake or real), decking, patio or gravel that we re-wild. Increasingly, our urban gardens are losing their ability to sequester carbon, provide habitat for wildlife and absorb water. This damages biodiversity and contributes both to the storm water overflows that pollute or flood our rivers, and to the lowering of the water table, amongst other things. But having wild-looking gardens is not acceptable to most people. In preparation for a talk I was giving, I came across a news story about someone being evicted for not taking care of their garden. There was a picture of the offending garden. It was not full of old mattresses and broken white goods. No. It was just overgrown. No chemicals had been used, and it must have provided a fantastic habitat for insects, small mammals and birds. But this was enough to get someone evicted. They would not have been evicted if they had used chemicals to kill everything off, covered it in black plastic underlay and gravel, and added a couple of pots of plastic flowers to make it look "pretty". It seems to me that there is something seriously wrong with our social norms around gardens, and it would be fantastic if we could set about changing those norms with a token scheme.

Counters

The mere act of counting has the potential for wider application. We could create challenges to count all sorts of things that would deliver benefits in both environmental and human terms. Some examples might be:

- Days without using your car; encouraging people to think twice before they use their car when there are alternatives that might just take a bit more effort.

- Self-propelled miles; encouraging people to walk or cycle, not just to save on CO_2 emissions or cut congestion, but also to improve health and wellbeing.

- The three-minute shower challenge; celebrating each day that people manage to have just one shower, and of only three minutes duration or less. This would not only save water; it would also save the energy that would have heated the additional water to 38 degrees.

- Days without using anything that comes with plastic packaging; encouraging people to think twice not just about single-use plastics, but, given the prevalence of packaging, their purchasing of stuff in general.

Each counter could have a running streak metric as well as a simple count. There could be anonymised league tables, enabling those of us who are driven by competition to see how we're doing compared to other people. For each activity counter, there would be information such as how many people in the city are signed up to try it, alongside some metrics about the impacts, for example, the estimated savings of water or energy use.

Of course, there is potential for people to over-report these counters. But I'm not particularly worried about that. First, there is no incentive for people to over-report. These points don't get you anything; they are worthless in market terms. Over-reporting would be like shaking your Fitbit to make it think you've done more steps than you have. There's very little point in doing that, and the few people who did would not have a negative effect on the overall benefits to people's health that Fitbits enable. Or it would be as if on social media you set up several accounts just so that you could like all your own posts and boost your engagement statistics. You wouldn't make yourself any happier, nor would you have any new friends. Even your real friends would probably soon start to wonder what was going on. So yes, the overall number of days without using cars might be overstated, for example, but the overall aim is to build momentum around the idea of not using your car, to normalise thinking twice before you start the engine, just because it will save you five minutes or mean you don't have to take an umbrella. From this perspective, a bit of over-reporting doesn't really matter.

In the longer term, when (in my utopian future) current-sees are being used as a governance process for managing the planetary commons, such a lax approach to counting would not be appropriate. But at this point, Bristol Pay would just be an experiment in using current-sees to motivate people to change their behaviours, so it's less of an issue.

Re-use Tokens

Re-use tokens would be assigned to physical things. Anyone could create a token to represent a thing they own that they want to share or give away. For example, I might create a token for my tent, my power drill, or a fancy-dress costume. These are items I don't use often and that, if I shared them or passed them on, could be better employed.

When I was thinking about re-use tokens, I came across an interesting statistic. Apparently, the average power drill is used for just four minutes before it ends up at the dump. This sounds crazy, right? Who would buy a power drill, use it to drill holes for putting up some shelves, and then take it straight to the dump? Of course, nobody does that. What they do is drill the holes, put up the shelves, and then put the power drill in the loft or garage. Some years later, when they want to put up some more shelves or whatever, one of several things is likely to happen. They might not be able to find the drill they seem to remember buying years ago, and so buy a new one, and when they come to move house some years later, the older drill will get thrown out. Or they might find the drill but discover it has seized up because it's not been used, and throw it out. They might even remember their old drill but be so impressed by the adverts for the latest cord-free drill (with amazing hammer action that doubles as a power screwdriver) that they go and buy themselves a swanky new one. As and when they come across the old drill, it will be chucked out. In all these cases, the original drill was only used for four minutes before it was ultimately thrown away.

The materials and energy used to create the power drill, not to mention the power taken to distribute it via warehouses—and perhaps via a shop—to your home are considerable. For all of this to enable a four-minute lifetime is an outrageous waste. It's true that too many tools are not built with longevity and repairability in mind, but most power tools have been designed to cope with more than four minutes of usage. To make the most of the resources invested in each piece of equipment we use, we should at least try to make sure it performs as much useful work as possible. If we can't use it ourselves, we could share it with friends and neighbours. Or we could give it away, perhaps using a site like Olio or Trash Nothing. We could donate it to a library of things—which operates like a normal library for books, but enables people to borrow equipment instead of books—through which many people will be able to have access to it.

The idea of the re-use token is that it would be passed on with the item each time it is lent or given to a new user or owner, and a counter on that token would be increased by one each time the item changes hands. I can imagine a league table of power drills based on the number of times each drill had been shared and used. This would serve to celebrate the sharing activity that had avoided the purchase of new drills, and that had thus saved the resources that would otherwise have been used in producing new drills. The token could also have markers showing how many times the item has been mended, to create visibility of the importance of repairing things.

I talked to one of the leading suppliers of software for libraries of things, and asked if they would be interested in linking their database to a tokenised blockchain. They were keen. I can imagine Trash Nothing and Olio also having the ability to associate a token with each listing. Charity shops might also get involved. The eventual aim would be that anyone wanting to borrow a power drill could search the blockchain and see where one was available near them, whether on Trash Nothing, at a charity shop or at a local library of things.

Voting Tokens

One of the most exciting ideas for tokens that we had was to create voting tokens. We have a problem in our society: most people are too busy to attend the annual general meetings (AGMs) of their local charities and community organisations. The majority don't even see the point in voting in local elections. As a result, the very people who are trying to serve our communities are doing so without any real understanding of how those living there are feeling. The only people they hear from are those few who feel engaged in the current system.

This growing disconnect between people and the organisations and institutions that exist to serve them is creating feelings of apathy and even outright distrust. The results can be seen in things like the rise of Donald Trump and the Brexit vote, where there is a move to overthrow the establishment, even though there is little understanding of what the alternative will really mean. Politics has become increasingly polarised, with the re-emergence in many parts of the world of populist movements, fuelled by a rhetoric of fear and mistrust, often directed against long-standing institutions that have been founded on principles of social justice.

If we are to create a peaceful world and a global commons economy, we need a way to engage people in decision making and to empower those who feel excluded. We need to do this early on so that people are not presented with simplified dichotomies that create instability. A commons economy will depend on surfacing shared concerns, and on building consent for courses of action to address those concerns.

We saw voting tokens as a small step in this direction. Any group or organisation could recognise various groups of stakeholders (local residents, staff, or beneficiaries of services, for example) and award those groups specific voting tokens. Any decision that needs to be taken could then be opened up to the relevant stakeholders. Rather than just framing decisions as yes or no, or option one, two or three, voting tokens would enable spread voting. This would create ratings of things that are important in making the decision. The aim would be to better understand how people are feeling about things, in turn enabling groups to come up with more nuanced approaches to solving problems. Meanwhile, with repeated voting or engagement exercises, stakeholders are taken on a journey, through which they can see why solutions are more complicated than they might think, and why there is a need to compromise if we are to build a peaceful society in which various needs can be met equitably. By looking at the history of their own voting token, people would be able to see what votes they had participated in, how their vote was spread across various types of concern, and how the overall vote was spread, in turn helping them understand others in their community and feel part of a truly consensual decision-making process.

Of course, we wanted the development of Bristol Pay tokens themselves (beyond the first few developed in advance to launch the product) to be determined through this sort of voting token.

CHAPTER NINE
THE FINAL ATTEMPT TO BRING BRISTOL PAY TO LIFE

In which we finally say goodbye

As we worked with Nathan and the team on creating a prototype that could explain our ideas in simple show-and-tell terms, it became clear that we'd have to narrow down all these token ideas to formulate a realistic minimum viable product (MVP) that we could put forward as a proposition to fund. The prototype itself needed to be simplified too, so that we could afford it within our limited budget. Finally, in November 2021, we had a basic version to show off. We held an event and invited all the potential partners and funders we could think of.

We had already been applying for funding to the larger trusts and foundations, trying to explain the entire concept, but had been rejected by all of them. The main problem was that potential funders wanted to know who our beneficiaries were and how we would be making an impact for them. This was tricky. Arguably, the beneficiaries were potentially everyone; the world would be a safer, more sustainable place if we could lessen our burden on nature and develop more social cohesion. The users were just a subset of the beneficiaries.

VALUE BEYOND MONEY

The fact that in the longer term there was still the plan to add a payment method to raise funds for the voluntary sector also made things trickier. There were just too many moving parts for funders to understand what we were trying to do.

With this in mind, we hoped we would identify some key partners at this November event so that we could write, say, half a dozen smaller funding applications with different partners, and thus raise enough funds between them to develop the platform. This way we could align ourselves with specific outcomes and groups of beneficiaries. We developed working relationships with Peter Bradley at UWE (the University of the West of England, providing some academic rigour to our ideas), with Bristol Water (focusing on cutting water usage), and Bristol Waste (with a view to reducing landfill waste). We were also talking to Avon Wildlife Trust about ways to encourage the re-wilding of gardens across Bristol, and to a variety of other third sector organisations across the city to whom we felt could provide engagement and impact measurement tools through the use of tokens. Some of these relationships got us to the point of submitting funding bids, with different outcomes and beneficiaries based on the partner(s) we were working with. But none were successful.

Things were getting desperate and innovative approaches were needed. This prompted me to put in one funding application saying that the key target audience was affluent people, as they were the ones who most needed to change their behaviour for the good of humanity. They, after all, were the people using the most resources and creating the greatest footprint. As you might guess, the idea of any charitable trust or foundation funding something that would be used by the most affluent people in society was soon proven to be laughable, but it was worth a shot.

Developing a Governance Structure

Alongside the work on developing our ideas for tokens, we started to think in earnest about what the governance structure of Bristol Pay should be. We sought to build in the potential for the project to be replicated in different cities from the outset, and we wanted to choose a legal structure that would make it immune to being hijacked by people who might see a potential to develop it for commercial purposes. This was a real concern. I had many conversations with people who could see that the tokens could become marketing tools for businesses, and were keen to fund us on that basis. Somehow, we needed to ensure that, should angel investors be found, they would see this as a philanthropic project that required patient capital rather than an opportunity to get a seat on the board and subvert the scheme to get themselves a return on their investment.

In the spring of 2022, I was lucky enough to get a place on Unfound, an incubator course for platform co-op startups. This was instrumental in helping us to come up with a potential future governance structure.

The main platform we would call City Pay. This would have a cooperative structure with several different classes of members, who would each have different rights. Classes would include investors, local implementations and staff. Whilst investor members, who would own withdrawable community shares, could have some voting rights, the majority of those rights would be held by the local implementations and staff. As the number of local implementations grew, the balance of power would shift towards them and away from the staff members.

The local implementations would be set up as community benefit societies (CBSs). These are a form of cooperative structure that is appropriate for non-profit organisations. The members of the CBS are not the beneficiaries; rather, all members of the community are beneficiaries. The members of the CBS, the people and groups with accounts on the system, would vote based on maximising benefits for the community. CBSs can also hold restricted funds, making them an ideal legal form for passing on any funds generated by the payment platform to local voluntary organisations. Distribution of money would be determined by members' votes (using our voting tokens, of course).

We started to develop governance rules for the platform co-op itself and for the CBSs. The idea was that the local implementations wanting to join would have to adopt the model rules, making sure that wherever the system was operating, the objectives and principles behind the implementation were safeguarded. In this respect, the structure would be like a franchise, with all the local implementations having the same objectives and structure, and agreeing to use the same branding, marketing and voting systems.

Funding for the Common Good

Based on this governance model, we developed a pitch deck for investors keen to put money into a project that would serve the common good. We wanted to be up front about the sorts of investors we were looking for; namely, people who desired to be part of a highly innovative and transformational project. We needed people who were happy to invest for the long term and who were not driven by the prospect of a financial return on their investment.

The process took several months, identifying the people we would approach and developing the deck, and to be (according to Rick Chapman, our entrepreneur in residence on the SETsquared team) "investor ready".

We had one response from someone asking for more information. After a couple of emails to and fro, explaining the whole City Pay proposal in more detail, even this potential investor backed away, saying we should be seeking grant funding rather than investment. But of course, we'd already exhausted the grant funding route. We now had just a few months of money left to try and pull in the funding to create Bristol Pay.

Academia

In early 2022, I was contacted by Marcus Petz, a PhD student who was keen to present some work at academic conferences and to get some papers published. He asked if I would be prepared to work with him, with the intention of co-writing some presentations and papers focusing on the achievements of Bristol Pound and the potential of Bristol Pay. I had recently had a conversation with a fundraiser from Oxfam, who had suggested that the reason trusts and foundations weren't prepared to fund our work was that it was too experimental. He recommended instead that we frame our work as action research and position ourselves as an alternative economy think tank. He felt that universities might be a potential source of funding for an action research project. As a result, when Marcus contacted me, I jumped at the opportunity. We wrote and submitted abstracts to the Global Conference on Economic Geography (GCEG), to be held in Dublin in early June 2022, and to the European Society for Ecological Economics (ESEE) conference in Pisa that would take place the following week. The abstract for the GCEG conference focused on the development of the Bristol Pay tokens, whilst for the ESEE we wrote mainly about the learnings from the Bristol Pound. We were accepted for both. We then got to work writing our joint conference papers and presentations.

To minimise our carbon footprint, we decided to travel by land and sea—a decision that meant that the travelling took over ten times as long and cost ten times more than flying. But luckily there was still enough money in the bank for us to be able to make that choice. It seemed a crazy venture; two weeks of travelling and attending presentations that I barely understood, just to speak a couple of times for ten or fifteen minutes about the work of the organisation. But it would all be worth it if it meant we got some research funding.

I was pleasantly surprised to have several interesting conversations with a range of academics, even though I felt like an imposter in their world. Many were very excited about the potential of funding PhD studies on the proposed new platform. Would it change behaviours? Would it create meaningful impacts? Were current-sees a useful way to track non-financial values? However, none of them had funding to put into the platform itself. It turns out universities are happy to fund developments that might accrue financial returns through intellectual property rights, but not otherwise. It was so frustrating. If each university had been prepared to put in just £10k or £20k, we could build the platform and they could have some exciting work for their PhD students. But it was not to be.

Subsequently, Marcus also successfully submitted an abstract to the Research Association on Monetary Innovation and Community and Complementary Currency Systems (RAMICS) conference in the autumn of 2022, but by this stage Bristol Pay had run out of funds, so he had to deliver that presentation alone.

The Last Fish

There was one other thing keeping me busy during the spring and early summer of 2022. I had been wondering what to do with all the unused 2018 series Bristol Pound notes that were still taking up space in my flat. In late 2021, the board had suggested that I ask all the artists who had been involved in designing the notes whether they had any good ideas for destroying them as part of an artistic event or installation. We wanted to create a project that would simultaneously draw attention to the work of the organisation and underline the ongoing need to rethink our economic system.

A few ideas came back, but one stood out. This came from Mary Collett, who designed the beautiful fox on the 2018 £B10 note. Her idea would involve lots of people, in particular children. It would use the notes creatively, and it would provide a fantastic opportunity to explain our concerns to Bristolians and visitors to the city. Her idea was to pitch to be part of the planned "Think Global Act Bristol" exhibition at M Shed in the summer of 2022, with an installation called "The Last Fish", inspired by Alanis Obomsawin's aforementioned quote.

The project would involve children cutting paper Bristol Pounds into fish shapes. Schools would be provided with Bristol Pounds and with two sets of lesson resources, one specifically for art lessons, and the other to help teachers to facilitate a wider class discussion on the global market economy and its impacts. The aim was to get 10,000 fish in the installation.

The pitch was successful. Mary and I wrote the lesson resources between us, with Mary focusing on the resources for art lessons, and I on the wider economics lessons. Meanwhile, we ran a publicity campaign and managed to get twenty-three schools signed up, along with some after-school clubs and brownie groups. It was a mammoth effort getting the notes out to schools, then collecting the finished fish back and delivering them to Mary. She and the team at M Shed got them all stuck onto netting and hung in the foyer, just in time for the launch of the exhibition.

The project was also captured on video, thanks to David Mathias. The film, which is still on the Bristol Pound YouTube channel, included footage from a class in one of the participating schools, with children discussing concepts such as whether money can buy love or happiness.

On the launch day, there was a heat wave. The glue failed and shoals of fish fell to the floor. It seemed very meta somehow that global warming was destroying our paper fish exhibition about the negative environmental effects of our economic system.

Over the next couple of weeks, Steven Bradley at M Shed, Mary, myself and Hector gave up every spare minute to slave over netting with hot glue guns, sticking the fish back on and getting a few burns in the process.

The final event

In July 2022, the board reluctantly had to take the decision to cease operations. The plan was that we'd hold a final conference and party, then make Hector and myself (as the last two remaining employees) redundant. Any leftover funds would be used to keep the website going as long as possible, just in case someone came out of the woodwork wanting to fund us.

The summer and early autumn of 2022 were spent planning the conference. Hector came up with the title "Way Out Economics", suggesting both that the ideas being discussed were pretty wacky, and that we were looking for a way out of the current economic system. I was approached by Dave Darby, a friend from the FIL fellowship, about the possibility of Credit Commons Society (CCS) co-hosting the event. This was great, as it was going to be a lot to organise between myself and Hector. Tom Woodroof did much of the work on behalf of the CCS, and my friend Kyle Wesley also got involved as a volunteer on the Bristol Pay side.

We wanted the conference to be a sort of un-conference. Rather than everyone showing off their wonderful projects and talking assuredly about their tried and tested approaches, I wanted people to share their wildest untested ideas. Whilst I was going to be the hostess and anchor person, introducing the day and the speakers and keeping time, I wasn't going to be talking very much about Bristol Pound or Bristol Pay. I figured that most of the people coming would have already heard me speak at length on those topics, but I knew they hadn't heard each other. I endeavoured to create a space where people could be brave enough to share their emerging thoughts. To bring together many of the people I'd talked to over the previous four years and enable a collaborative and generative discussion.

Through CCS, I was introduced to Francois Knuchel, who provided extensive expertise in designing and facilitating the conference. We came up with a format: three speakers presenting their own "provocations" for ten minutes each, followed by half an hour of open space discussions, repeated four times throughout the day. There would also be a troika session, through which small groups of people could support each other as peer consultants.

We put out a call for provocations. We had far more responses than we could fit into the day, and made selections of who would speak on the basis of how unusual but well formulated the ideas were. We grouped the speakers into themes, starting with ideas to improve the market economy, and moving towards non-market approaches later in the day.

We decided early on that we wanted the event to be fully hybrid, as the people I had been speaking to were based all over the UK and beyond. Thanks to Luke John Emmett and the team at Spirolux, we were able to achieve this, with Zoom rooms for online attendees running in parallel to the open space sessions at the main venue. Some provocations were from people attending in person, whilst others were from online attendees. Everything went extremely smoothly, and the feedback showed that people had found the day really inspiring. We created an information-sharing resource so that attendees could keep in contact with each other after the event, and I know of a few collaborations that took off as a result of the conference. I could not have wished for more.

The day culminated with a tenth birthday party for the Bristol Pound. The conference attendees were invited, along with key supporters of the Bristol Pound currency since its early days. I got to dance with the late and much-missed Michael Hallam, with whom I had spent so much time in Zoom meetings since the first lockdown, forever discussing how to change the man-made systems that control our lives—from the economy to education—and how to build the connections, relationships, and spiritual growth that would enable those changes to occur. Then there were speeches and votes of thanks. The whole day was exhilarating; one of the best of my life.

The End

After the conference, I gradually found homes for all the Bristol Pound kit in my flat. The last remaining notes were shredded (apart from a few for ongoing souvenir sales), the IT equipment was collected to be wiped of data and given away to new homes. The website was kept going for a few months, and the writing of this book started with the board's blessing. Finally, the board took the decision to wind up the company in spring 2023, and entrusted me with its legacy.

The process of gradually saying goodbye to the most important job of my life stretched out over many months and has been a painful process. Winding up the company felt like a bereavement.

I don't know what the future will hold. But then again, who does? I really hope to find a way to continue what I feel is the urgent work of developing experiments that could help us design a global commons economy. I also hope that this book and the work of the organisation I loved so much will inspire others to do the same.

ACRONYMS

AML - Anti Money Laundering

B2B - Business to Business

BBC - British Broadcasting Corporation

BCU - Bristol Credit Union, since renamed to be Great Western Credit Union

BNI - Business Network International

CBS - Community Benefit Society

CCS - Credit Commons Society

CEO - Chief Executive Officer

CIC - Community Interest Company

CND - Campaign for Nuclear Disarmament

COP15 - 15th Session of the Conference of the Parties to the United Nations Framework Convention on Climate Change

DIY - Do It Yourself (home maintenance)

EMI - Electronic Money Institution

ESEE - European Society for Ecological Economics

EU - European Union

FCA - Financial Conduct Authority

FIL - Finance Innovation Lab

FSA - Financial Services Authority

GCEG - Global Conference on Economic Geography

GDPR - General Data Protection Regulation

GOIC - Guild of Independent Currencies

HR - Human Resources

IMA - Independent Money Alliance

ISM - Individual, Social and Material

KYC - Know Your Customer

LED - Light Emitting Diode

LETS - Local Exchange Trading System

P4NE - Partners for a New Economy

RAMICS - Research Association on Monetary Innovation and Community and Complementary Currency Systems

REC - Real Economy Currency

RWA - Royal West of England Academy

SDG - United Nations Sustainable Development Goals

SEMI - Small Electronic Money Institution

SMS - Short Message Service

STrO - Social Trade Organisation (owners of Cyclos)

TLA - Three Letter Acronym!

UBI - Universal Basic Income

USA - United States of America

USP - Unique Selling Point

UWE - University of the West of England

VAT - Value Added Tax

VIP - Very Important Person

XR - Extinction Rebellion

INDEX

access to digital money 147

alternative economy 166, 172

behaviour change 182, 189

blockchain 127, 129, 154

Brixton Pound 20

carbon trading 159

circular economy 169, 178

closed loop 144

commons 160, 165, 172

community wealth building 17, 21, 46, 107

consumer debt 4

credit clearing circle 32

crypto-currencies 130

current-sees 173, 190

earn and spend 9, 13, 196

environmental capital 175

expiry date 100

externalities 158

financial economy 162

fintech 21, 47, 115

fungible 174

gamified 190, 192

intellectual property 178, 213

interest-free 70, 120

inward investment 21

land ownership 176, 179

leakage 22

legal tender 15, 42, 99

LETS 9, 20, 32

localisation 16, 107 138

local multiplier 22, 138

manufactured capital 178

multiple capital 176

mutual credit 12, 32, 33

net zero carbon 167, 186

new economy 166

non-financial value 173, 193, 212

nudge economics 182

payment cards 103, 156

push payment 105

ratio of reserves to deposits 119

real economy 89, 162

real value 158, 173

scope one, two and three emissions 167

social capital 10, 177

social justice 14, 54, 133, 171

social media 189

timebanking 9, 20

tipping points 187

token design 154

Totnes Pound 20

town pound 20, 22, 27

tragedy of the commons 160

Transition Network 20

velocity 11, 22

women's work 164

FURTHER READING

A selection of books, some read and recommended by me, others read and recommended by people I've interviewed whilst writing this book (and that I'm adding to my own reading list).

Before Babylon, Beyond Bitcoin: From Money that We Understand to Money that Understands Us, by David Birch

Braiding Sweetgrass, by Robin Wall Kimmerer

Bullshit Jobs, by David Graeber

Cloudmoney: Cash, Cards, Crypto and the War for Our Wallets, by Brett Scott

Doughnut Economics, by Kate Raworth

Freakonomics: A Rogue Economist Explores the Hidden Side of Everything, by Steven Levitt and Stephen Dubner

Governing the Commons, by Elinor Ostrom

Limits to Growth: The 30-Year Update, by Donella Meadows and Jorgen Randers

Sacred Economics: Money, Gift and Society in the Age of Transition, by Charles Eisenstein

Shut Down the Business School: What's Wrong with Management

Education, by Martin Parker

Small is Beautiful, by EF Schumacher

Tescopoly, by Andrew Simms

The Dawn of Everything, by David Graeber and David Wengrow

The Death and Life of the Great American Cities, by Jane Jacobs

The Future is Degrowth: A Guide to a World beyond Capitalism, by M Schmelzer, A Vetter and A Vansintjan

The Irrational Bundle: Predictably Irrational, The Upside of Irrationality, and The Honest Truth About Dishonesty, by Daniel Ariely

Thinking, Fast and Slow, by Daniel Kahneman

Tipping Point, by Malcolm Gladwell

Trekonomics: The Economics of Star Trek, by Manu Saadia

ACKNOWLEDGMENTS

This list is very long.

First, I would like to thank my family and close friends who have been with me on my journey of discovery. My mother, Anne Curry, and my late father, Tony Curry, who instilled in me early on the ideas of service and community value. My big sisters, Gill Rapley and Sue Flanagan, who have been constants in my life, shaping my development and always being good audiences for my emerging ideas. My ex-husband, Jonny Finch, who put up with me during my lowest phases as I tried to understand my place in the world, and gave me two fantastic children. My two daughters, Abi Finch and Bet Finch, who are an inspiration to me every day with their energy and love of people and planet, sustained despite the difficult trajectory we are all on. My aunt Eve Jackson, who has introduced me to so many ideas both spiritual and intellectual. My aunt Mave Ersu, who was a big influence in developing my sense of humour, so vital in this serious work. Xavier de la Huerga, without whom I would never have come across the idea of challenging our economic system. My thanks also to the many friends who have been important in my life as I've been writing this, including Gene Joyner, Jon Eldridge, Kat Tudor, Kathy Morris and Monique Johnstone.

Next, I'd like to thank all the people that made my job at the Bristol Pound the best I've ever had. I'll start with the people who so kindly agreed to be interviewed for this book, and who put in so much time and energy into the project, often unpaid: the founders, Chris Sunderland, Ciaran Mundy, David Hunter, Mark Burton and Steve Clarke, who had such vision and bravery; James Berry, who collaborated with us so whole-heartedly; Bobbie Sunderland, Graham Woodruff, Jen Green, Katie Finnegan-Clarke, Mike Lloyd-Jones and Sarah Forrester, who were central to making things happen; George Ferguson, who shared our vision and promoted our ideas for so many years; and Ben Heald, who, as chair, offered me the job, and supported me through thick and thin.

There are many whom I didn't interview but who have also been key. On the board, I'd like to thank Mike Cranney and Sally Britton for their support, and Farid Tejani for sharing so many ideas that were central to the Bristol Pay project. I'd like to thank my colleagues Hector Steenbergen, Ian Madle and Nic Hemley, who were constantly inspiring to me. My thanks, too, to the many other staff, board members and volunteers that I've left out of this book, but who gave so much to the organisation at various points along the way.

I'd like to thank the organisations that have generously supported my learning, in particular the Finance Innovation Lab, the MetaCurrency Project and Unfound. Without their courses, I would not have been introduced to many of the ideas that have influenced my thinking.

Huge thanks to the many people who have inspired and influenced the development of my thinking. These include Alex Booth, Alex Merron, Andrew Darnton, Dil Green, Donnie Maclurcan, Grace Rachmany, Henry Leveson-Gower, John Wood, Kostas Iatridis, Kyle Wesley, Marcus Petz, Mark Thurstain-Goodwin, Martin Parker, Michael Hallam, Michael

Johnson, Peter Bradley, Toby Harris and Zaid Hassan, though this is not an exhaustive list. Over the course of the last five years, thanks to the reputation of the Bristol Pound, I've been privileged to have conversations with many interesting and enlightened people from all over the world about how we can change our economic system. I can't possibly list them all, but they have all helped shape my thoughts in countless ways, and I thank them all heartily for their passion and generosity.

Finally, special thanks to Steve Mcnaught and the Arkbound Foundation for encouraging me to write this book and for publishing it, to all who supported the crowdfunder that enabled it to be published, and to the many people who have spent so much time reading and refining my early drafts.